TRADE UNIONS AND THE MEDIA

Edited by
Peter Beharrell
and
Greg Philo

© Francis Beckett, Peter Beharrell, J. Brooke Crutchley,
Howard Davis, Peter Golding, Andrew Goodman,
Toni Griffiths, John Hewitt, Tony Marshall,
Graham Murdock, Greg Philo, Alan Sapper,
Paul Walton, Jock Young 1977

First edition 1977
Reprinted 1978

Published by
THE MACMILLAN PRESS LTD
London and Basingstoke
Associated companies in Delhi Dublin
Hong Kong Johannesburg Lagos Melbourne
New York Singapore and Tokyo

Printed in Hong Kong

British Library Cataloguing in Publication Data

Trade unions and the media. – (Critical social studies).
1. Mass media and trade unions – Great Britain
I. Beharrell, Peter   II. Philo, Greg   III. Series
301.5'5   P96.T/

ISBN 0–333–22055–2

Contents

Acknowledgements

We would like to thank our colleagues of the Glasgow University Media Group for their help and advice, especially those who are not directly involved in this volume but who helped all the same, Jean Oddie, Professor J. E. T. Eldridge and Brian Winston.

There were many other friends who encouraged us in this and other projects by endlessly listening and advising, in particular Mike Gonzales, Mae Boyd, Susan Golombok, Des McNulty, Dave Frisby, Colin Filer, Jenny Buchanan, Margaret Chroston, Alex Graham, Ravi Rana, Bert Moorhouse, Mark Piney, Lynne Jones, Hugh Richards, Susan Baird, John Cudmore, Paul Gordon, Roger Levy, Dougie Allen, Neil Williamson, Trevor Pateman, Stuart Hall, Ian Connell and Dave Morley. Thanks to our many friends in the trade union movement who helped us with criticisms and comments and by organising meetings and discussion groups, especially Jimmy Milne, Gordon Craig, Jimmy Kirkwood, Ken McMillan, Eddie Myles, Ian McDonald, Alec Murray, Geoffrey Drain, Steven White, George Munt, Dave Smith, Margaret Boyle and Bob Harrison, and also John Leopold and Simon Henderson of the Workers' Educational Association in Scotland.

There are many friends inside the media we must thank, especially Gillian Skirrow and all those who worked on *Viewpoint*; also Brian Barr and Ron MacKay in Glasgow and Shaie Selzer of Macmillan.

Thanks to Margaret Hall and Pru Larsen of Glasgow University, and Patricia Kelly who typed the manuscript. Special thanks are due to Rene and Dick Philo and their home for damaged academics and to Stella 'Scoop' McGarritty for assisting with the research.

Introduction

This collection of essays is about the mass communications system of our society. It deals with the ownership and control of the mass media and the kind of messages that it broadcasts and prints. The common interest of the contributors here is in how the organisation of the media, and what it produces, reflects the power of dominant interests in society at large.

Throughout history, ruling groups have sought to justify their power with the claim that the existing social relationships work to the mutual benefit of all. While political power has often grown from the barrels of guns, there have also been attempts to strengthen it by the control of ideas, beliefs and values. The mass media now play a crucial role in the battle of ideas, over what is held by people to be important, necessary or possible within society. There is the well-known story of Alexander the Great and Napoleon watching the May Day Parade in Moscow. Alexander was transfixed by the sight of the huge nuclear missiles and said, 'With arrows like that I could have conquered the world.' Napoleon had not bothered to watch the parade and had merely flicked through the pages of *Pravda*. 'But with newspapers like these', he said, 'no one would have heard of Waterloo.'

This volume focuses on the control of ideas, information and explanations in our own society. It is a society which is deeply divided over the ownership of property and wealth, and a society characterised by great inequalities of power which flow from these fundamental divisions. One aspect of this inequality is that the broadcasting institutions and the Press are in the hands of a very small number of people. The dimension of the ownership and control of the media is documented in this volume by Graham Murdock and Peter Golding. A further dimension to the study of communications is the analysis of dominant ideas and values as they appear in news reports, in Press and television coverage. A society based on power and private property might be expected to generate serious conflicts. This is especially so in the area of industrial life, between those who own and control economic production, and those whom they employ. It is now almost commonplace to say that the media view the world through spectacles tinted with 'consensual values'. That is, they present and describe a social system based upon private interest as if in its normal workings it will somehow automatically benefit everyone who is a part of it. Yet the history of that system has been one of savage and harsh conflict in the struggle to achieve the most basic social rights and liberties. Jock Young and J. Brooke Crutchley in their article show how the media brush this history aside in order to present conflicts over social and political ends as the agitation of an irrational minority.

The point to which we draw attention in our study here is that the 'normal' workings of a specific social and economic system are never presented as if they could generate serious problems. When crisis and serious conflict do strike the system, they are treated in the media as an aberration, and frequently as resulting from the 'dark motives' of selected individuals. The favourite scapegoats here, of course, are trade unionists, and, as we show in our study, problems which result from the manner in which the economic system is organised are most likely to be laid at their door.

There are many people in the trade unions who in their day-to-day work are involved in trying to change this picture. Toni Griffiths and Francis Beckett, as union press officers, draw from their experience to give an account of the difficulties of combating the power of the dominant and 'official' views. There are also those who work to produce an alternative viewpoint within trade union publications. Tony Marshall in his article shows the gaps between the portrayal of farmworkers in the public Press, and the realities of their struggle for a living wage.

Some journalists inside the media institutions strive to give alternative viewpoints. The pressures to conform to the establishment view and to 'behave' are great, however, and Andrew Goodman illustrates some of them from his own experience and from that of others within the media. From the viewpoint and experience of the television workers, Alan Sapper describes the attempts to create a more open and democratic medium in terms of both its internal structures and its responsibility to the wider public.

In the last few essays of the collection, Graham Murdock and Peter Golding, and some of the members of the Glasgow Media Group, Paul Walton and Howard Davis, give an account of the progress of research and the contentious public debate on the future of the media.

PETER BEHARRELL
GREG PHILO

1

One-dimensional News – Television and the Control of Explanation

GREG PHILO
Lecturer in Sociology, University of Glasgow

PETER BEHARRELL
Research Officer, University of Glasgow

JOHN HEWITT
Lecturer in Sociology, Liverpool College of Higher Education

The lamps in Parliament Square glister across the Thames, the camera moves to Big Ben, a close-up, it's ten o'clock – Bong! – the familiar voice of Reginald Bosanquet – 'M.P.'s pay rise endangers Social Contract' – Bong! – 'Royal Family squares up for massive wage claim' – Bong! – 'British Leyland's future threatened by huge dividend payouts' – Bong! – 'Traffic to be disrupted by Queen's Procession'.

All of these headlines relate to news stories that have been reported on the television news, but this was not exactly the manner in which they were presented. Yet some news stories did appear in this way. We were in fact told that the Social Contract was 'threatened'. Not, however, by the pay claims of M.P.s, hospital consultants or the Queen, but by those of miners, engineering workers and dockers. Similarly we were told that the traffic in London was going to be 'disrupted'. The cause of this was not, however, a Royal Procession but a trade union demonstration in support of the jailed Shrewsbury pickets.

The way in which stories are presented thus affects how the events to which they refer are to be seen and understood. Television news, like all journalism, never simply gives 'the facts' but always offers us a way of understanding the world in which we live. Television is the main source of news for over half the population (according to the programme *Inside the News*, B.B.C. 1, 18 November 1974). Each night over twenty million people watch the main bulletins. Both the B.B.C. and I.T.N. are legally bound to accuracy, balance and impartiality, but a careful examination of how they actually present and report news stories shows that they describe the world in a very particular way. One dimension of this is the different status and treatment accorded to the views and actions of various social groups. For example, it is possible to point to the down-grading of rank-and-file dockers in news coverage and to the singling out of individuals for special treatment in this area. For example, during a dispute in the London docks in March 1975 I.T.N. gave this report.

And one of their strike leaders, in fact the man at the centre of the London Dock Strike, is Mr Brian Nicholson; a controversial figure during two dock meetings where the voting's been disputed. Geoffrey Archer reports:

Brian Nicholson has attracted the attention of the cameras only during the last few weeks as leader of the latest dock strike, but he's been a major political force in the docks for many years. In 1969 he was largely responsible for the Bristow Committee reporting on the ports; at the time their proposals were shelved and in 1972 when Bernie Steer and Vic Turner were briefly imprisoned for being in contempt of the Industrial Relations Court, *Nicholson was thought to be the master mind behind the dispute at the time.* He is Chairman of the Docks Group of the Transport and General Workers' Union. The recent disputes over who should run the Container Depots have been largely in the hands of the shop stewards, led by Vic Turner, *but in the last few weeks Nicholson has taken over,* in his role as local union chairman, even though the strike is unofficial. *This has been his bid for ultimate power in the London Docks.*

Brian Nicholson lives in Hackney; he's divorced and he has three children; he's a member of the Labour Party and of the National Executive of the Transport Union. For the four months prior to this dispute he's been on sick leave with an injured leg. Nicholson's main political affiliation is to the Institute for Workers' Control, an organisation based in Nottingham, which had the late Bertrand Russell as its honorary President. Nicholson is a Vice-Chairman of the Institute, whose members include the Minister of State for Northern Ireland, Mr Stan Orme, and whose Conference this year will be addressed by the Industry Secretary, Mr Tony Benn.

Brian Nicholson has written a number of pamphlets on the docks, urging total workers' control throughout Britain so that dock employees can have complete power to dictate terms and conditions of employment. *His involvement in recent days in disputed vote counting may have been a set-back to his ambition as a Dockers' leader.* (I.T.N. 2200 27 March 1975)

But hospital consultants are a very different kettle of agitators. For men such as these to be forced to work to rule – or work to contract in their case – there must be something very rotten indeed in the state of the Social Services Secretary. On the first day of the hospital consultants' work to rule in 1975, Robert Kee on *First Report* interviewed Barbara Castle. He began,

Mrs Castle, on the face of it this seems a terrible indictment of you as an employer that the very top people in the medical profession should be forced for the first time in history to take this action. (I.T.N. 1300 2 January 1975)

The private treatment that was extended to the hospital consultants, however, went beyond the idosyncrasies of Robert Kee. What we were shown was what a wonderful job the consultants did normally. The reporter Angela Lambert, for example, took us lyrically through the hospital wards, showing us how overworked and humane doctors are. Her account of a day in the life of a consultant began,

It's nine o'clock and the surgeon prepares for this morning's seven operations, four of them quite minor, and three, including one on this small boy, major and possibly

complicated. This theatre handles some 3000 operations a
year and Mr Rex Hunter performs about half of them,
working ten to twelve hours a day, never less than six days a
week. Finally the unconscious child gets his panda back.
(I.T.N. 2200 1 January 1975)

It would be difficult to imagine a similar day-in-the-life
reported in other contexts, such as a strike in a coal mine or a
car plant. Not only was the humanity of consultants pointed
out but their long hours of devoted service. On the day their
dispute ended we were told,

> One of the most lasting effects of this whole dispute has
> been technically unforeseen. There's no doubt that during
> the last fifteen weeks many of the consultants have come to
> appreciate the extra time they have been able to devote to
> their private and social lives and whether the dispute is
> settled or not, many of these consultants will be reluctant to
> return to the sort of timetables that regularly require them
> to put in seventy hours work a week. (B.B.C. 1 2100 18
> April 1975)

Many people work long hours in our society. We wait in vain
for a report of the end of a miners' overtime ban telling us that
'many coal-face workers will be reluctant to return to the sort
of shifts that regularly require them to work in a dangerous
dusty atmosphere for a third of what a consultant earns'.
But criticism of 'imbalance' or 'bias' must go much deeper
than questions of who gets on or the status accorded to
different individuals or groups. In the end the argument is
really about the kind of world that those who construct the
news believe that they live in. It is a world that is populated by
inflationary wage claims, strikes and disruptions, and the
perpetual battle between the responsible majority and the
small minority who always want to spoil everything for the
rest of us. This is not intended as a list of everything media
journalists believe. What is crucial about these beliefs is that
they are the basis for the organisation and presentation of a
particular kind of news. They are at the heart of the information that is selected and reported on industrial life.

What we will illustrate here is more than the inclusion in news broadcasts of isolated examples of 'bias' in an otherwise 'neutral' or 'factual' coverage. For what is at stake here is the total organisation of coverage around assumptions of the nature of the social world and what moves it. Arguments about 'news bias' often become discussions of whether individuals or groups get a 'fair deal' in coverage. This is often pitched at the level of whether they are spoken of 'favourably' or 'unfavourably' and the search thus proceeds for evaluative language or 'emotive' expressions. But to do this is to miss the essential dimension of the control that media producers exercise over the explanation of social life and of what actions in society produce what effects.

The apparently routine reporting of 'facts', 'figures' and 'events' reveals the basic assumptions with which news is produced. For example, we analysed the T.V. news coverage of a strike of 250 engine tuners at British Leyland's Cowley plant which began in January 1975. In this news coverage there were many references to the production losses 'caused' by the strike. Figures for these were formulated in relation to a concept of 'normal' production. Thus we were told on I.T.N. that while the tuners were on strike, production continued at 80 per cent of 'normal'.

> For a week now the company has been keeping production up to eighty per cent of normal and stockpiling cars for the tuners to attend to when the dispute is settled. (I.T.N. 1300 20 January 1975)

And on B.B.C. 1, that,

> For the moment, at least, normal production of cars – Maxis and Marinas – 12,000 of which, worth about one and three-quarter million pounds, were lost yesterday – was possible. (B.B.C. 1 1745 January 1975)

What is crucial here is that normal production and full production are treated as synonymous by news journalist and are equated with production that is strike free. Hence, during a period of the dispute when the tuners temporarily returned to work, I.T.N. informed us that,

> With the engine-tuners back at work at least for the time being, the Austin Morris plant singled out by the Prime Minister for particular criticism was also back in full production. (I.T.N. 1300 7 January 1975)

And on B.B.C. 1,

> The engine-tuners at British Leyland's Cowley works have ended their strike and the plant is back in full production. (B.B.C. 1 1745 7 January 1975)

However, it was reported on 11 January by the *Guardian, Daily Telegraph, The Times* and the *Financial Times*, that in the period immediately before this, over half of the loss of production had nothing to do with disputes at Leyland. Four months later the government's Ryder report on British Leyland pointed to the chronic investment record of the company's management as a key factor leading to the car giant's decline. In particular Ryder criticised the management's decision to distribute 95 per cent of the firm's profits between 1968 and 1972 as dividends to shareholders and the retention of only 5 per cent for re-investment purposes. Leyland's profits between 1968 and 1972 had been £74 million – of this £70 million was distributed as dividends. One effect of this lack of investment was that a great part of British Leyland's plant and machinery was obsolete. The machinery frequently broke down and production was inefficient and uncompetitive. However, in news reports of British Leyland's troubles, phenomena such as mismanagement and machine failure were embodied within the 'normal', while the 'disruption' of the production process was an exclusive function of the activity of the workforce.

Thus a production stoppage becomes equated in general usage with a strike. Here, for example, a media reporter notes that stocks must be good in Chrysler because they say they have had a run without strikes,

With a touch of irony, Chrysler said that they have had a run without production stoppages, without strikes, so stocks must be good. But for all their optimism, the workforce is going on a three-day week for the rest of January. (B.B.C. 1 2100 9 January 1975)

Such is the pervasiveness of this account of the car industries' problems that it is introduced even when the immediate subject does not involve a description of an industrial dispute. Thus, it is used in this instance in the description of a new Leyland car that is about to be launched,

Onlookers outside the Cowley factory gates have been getting an unplanned preview of a new British Leyland car. It's the successor to the Austin 1800 range, code named 8071 and due to be launched in the spring, *strikes permitting*. British Leyland hope it will revive interest in their cars in a sagging home market. (B.B.C. 1 2100 9 January 1975) (our italics)

A more extensive account of this strike and its news coverage is given in the collected research findings of the Glasgow Media Group (*Bad News*, Routledge and Kegan Paul, 1976). In our case study of Leyland news coverage, we found that the problems of a particular industry are explained substantially as problems with the workforce. This is in part a question of some explanations being highlighted in the coverage relative to others. Some explanations are taken up directly by news journalists and are used as their own. In the case of the Leyland study, we found that this was done only with the 'strike' explanation of Leyland's problems. Thus we hear of the engine tuners' dispute that,

It's the kind of strike that has contributed significantly to the dire economic difficulties of British Leyland. (I.T.N. 2200 4 January 1975)

More importantly, the news is in a sense organised around such 'favoured' explanations. The focus of a large part of the news is on pursuing the logic and rationale of these chosen explanations. Thus when strikes are presented as the source of an industry's problems we know and are informed of exactly what strikes do. The resources of the media are organised to give us this information. We are regularly informed, for example, of how much lost production or damage is being 'caused' by the strike. We also know who is to 'blame' for this problem. Thus, a kind of causal chain is set up by which we know what a strike is, what it does, who it affects (the consumer and other workers), the damage it causes and who is to blame. News coverage is organised around such themes but no similar causal chain exists for other explanations of industrial crisis. There is no systematic explanation on the news of the system of private investment. References to this system as possibly generating problems, if they appear at all, occur only as fragments. Unless we are informed what under-investment means, what it causes and what has happened to the money that might have been invested, then such references as there *are* exist only at the level of disparate and fragmented pieces of information. This is partly because some links in the chain of explanation are missing because, for example, we are never informed as to the number of breakdowns and the loss of production due to obsolete machinery. Similarly, there is no routine coverage of the movement of investment capital, which has been a key factor in the decline of productive industry, of which British Leyland was only one example. There is no critical account, let alone routine referencing, of problems such as the export of private capital, or the movement of capital away from productive industry into various forms of profiteering such as speculation in land or commodities.

Such phenomena are simply not part of the routine organisation of news coverage. These explanations of economic life are not embraced as themes in reporting, and there is no search for their effects or causes. The 'normal' workings of a particular kind of economy, such as that of the United Kingdom, are not treated by the television news as if they might themselves generate serious problems. This is equally apparent if we turn to the manner in which the economy as a whole and its problems are described. As a part of our research study, we made a detailed analysis of the news coverage of the Social Contract over a four-month period, from January to April 1975. One of our central concerns was to examine who or what the media blamed for the economic crisis, and how this was linked to political solutions. This is of crucial importance, for it is obvious that the manner in which economic problems are explained will affect how people relate••• to different solutions. A simple example would be that if most people were convinced that inflation was caused by 'excessive' wage increases, then a policy of cutting wages to reduce inflation might appear as socially just and acceptable. If, however, it was argued that prices were rising because of 'excessive' profits or from the activities of speculators and financiers, then a policy of lowering wages to resolve the crisis might not have the same public approval and support.

In the period of our research, as now, there was a vigorous debate amongst both academic economists and in the society at large on what was wrong with Britain's economy and on how it could be put right. Much of this argument, as it was reported in the media, focused on what was causing inflation. There are a number of different areas of opinion on this. On the right wing of the political spectrum the Monetarists in the Conservative Party blamed primarily government expenditure and as a solution they called for it to be cut. Other groups blamed 'excessive' wage increases as the source of the problem and proposed wage restraint and the lowering of living standards as a solution. The most prominent political figures amongst these were Denis Healey and the Prime Minister. Support for their views came from the Treasury and the C.B.I. Opposition to these explanations of the problem came from a large section of the trade union movement and from the left of the Labour Party, notably the Tribune group. For these, the key factor in the economic crisis was the chronic investment record of private industry. For solutions they looked towards the National Enterprise Board and the expansion of the public sector.

There were many in the trade union movement who rejected outright the view that the economic crisis and inflation were the result of 'excessive' wage increases. In a letter to the *Guardian*, Geoffrey Drain, the General Secretary of NALGO, argued that the wages–inflation link is no more than a politically convenient cliche. Replying to a *Guardian* editorial he notes that,

> You go on to say that 'high unemployment today is substantially a reflection of excessive wage settlements yesterday'. Where is the argument to support this claim? Admittedly, it is a cliche we often hear from some politicians of a certain shade, yet never from economists of any repute . . . If the implicit argument behind the cliche quoted above is that the wage settlements caused by inflation caused (but again, how?) the unemployment, then where is the reference to the impact of monetary expansion in 1973, raw material and oil prices in 1973 and 1974, and the continual slide of sterling against other currencies? All of these contributed substantially to inflation, just as the Government's easing of the price code will next year, and none of these can be said to relate to wages in 1974 or 1975. (*Guardian* 8 September 1976)

There were other positions which were combinations of those outlined above. For example many trade unionists rejected the view that 'excessive' wages were the source of the problem, but none the less accepted the principles of limited wage restraint to help resolve the crisis.

There were thus many contending explanations for what was wrong with Britain's economy. Yet in the period of study, the complexities of inflation were reduced, on the news, substantially to the question of which trade unions were 'breaking' the Social Contract. The dominant theme of television news bulletins throughout the four-month period was the view that 'excessive' wage increases were the central problem, and this explanation and the political policies with which it was associated was consistently underlined and emphasised in the coverage. A simple numerical assessment of the references to the theme of 'excessive' wage increases as the source of the economic problem reveals that this far outnumbered any of the other explanations of crisis which were given on the television news at this time. This was at a period when the industrial editor of I.T.N. had commented in one bulletin that,

Since the war, Britain's overriding problem almost universally agreed *has been a failure to invest adequately*. Since 1969 the problem has become worse with investment increasing at nowhere near the rate of production. The result, machines increasingly out of date working at their limit and uncompetitive. 1975, to cap it all, now looks like being a year of huge investment collapse. (I.T.N. 2200 21 January 1975)

Yet overall in the news, references to wage increases as the central problem outnumbered references to investment by almost three to one. In the period of the study there were ninety-four references to the 'wage increases' and thirty-three to investment as key problems. These references occurred either as direct statements from media personnel or as reported statements which were included in news bulletins. A small number were made in interviews. The theme that wages were 'soaring' and that this was the key problem was consistently and systematically pursued by news journalists. Only eleven statements were included which disagreed with this view. At times the theme of wage increases as the central cause of crisis and inflation was linked directly by news journalists to the political policy of wage restraint. The industrial correspondent of the B.B.C. thus argued in January 1975 that,

With wages now as the main boost in inflation, just getting inflation down to a reasonable level seems to imply tougher pay restraint. A statutory wage policy is still officially ruled out, but one cannot help thinking despite Mr Healey's denials that between the lines of his speech ten days ago was a warning to unions that to insist on maintaining living standards might be asking too much. (B.B.C. 1 2100 20 January 1975)

There was no similar embracing or underlining of other political policies by the B.B.C. news.

Policies such as those of the Industry Bill which were designed to reverse the decline of investment received a quite different treatment on the news. There were forty-seven references to the need for more investment through the N.E.B. and the need for the government to reverse the downward trend of British industry. By comparison there were 289 references to the need for wage restraint and lower living standards. There were only seventeen references included criticising policies of wage restraint. It will be remembered that the Industry Bill was in fact opposed by powerful interests such as the C.B.I. Perhaps for this reason there were fifty references included critical of the policies of the Bill by comparison with the forty-seven references in favour of them.

Such numerical assessments give a broad indication of which political themes were dominant in news coverage. A more crucial dimension is the manner which the news is organised and presented to give credence and validity to some political explanations against others.

The key political explanation on the news was that wage increases had caused the inflationary crisis. Much of the news was organised to explore and give credence to this very partial view, and to its corollary that harsh deflationary policies were therefore necessary and in a sense 'inevitable'. The consequences of these policies are now well known with the large increase in unemployment that they produced. At the time of their introduction, for example, in the budget of April 1975, they were presented on the news as a 'necessary' response to the inflation that had been caused by trade union activity. When the budget appeared, it was introduced on the main news of I.T.N. as follows:

> Good evening. In the toughest of budgets the Chancellor, Mr Healey, has fired a broadside at *all those who had taken high pay rises. These, he said, were the main cause of the present rate of inflation*. (I.T.N. 2200 15 April 1975)

The rationale of alternative points of view on the budget was substantially ignored. For example, both the Tribune group and a large section of the trade union movement were opposed at this time to the deflationary measures of the budget on the grounds that their consequences would be further heavy unemployment and recession. Their views were drawn from the Keynesian principle that economic slumps are caused by the mass of the population having insufficient income to buy back the commodities that they have produced. They were thus opposed to the government cutting back its spending and to the lowering of income by increased taxation. There was no sense in which the news was organised to give credence or coherence to such views. They were referenced on the news but there was no sense in which the news was organised to explore and justify their rationale and logic. For example, in the following instance, the B.B.C. economic correspondent gives a long exposition of Mr Healey's views, and then the Tribune group is briefly mentioned,

> If we don't tighten our belts the implication is foreign creditors from whom we borrow will insist that we do before they lend us any more. Without more modest wage deals and better productivity on the shop floor Mr Healey says our prices will soon be rising twice as fast as those of our competitors. So his message called for belt-tightening and the party meeting *rejected a call from the left-wing Tribune group for an opposite give-away budget*. This afternoon M.P.s were gloomily forecasting higher income tax in the April budget as the only alternative to politically impossible statutory wage policy. (B.B.C. 1 2100 19 March 1975)

To reduce this alternative view to 'a call for an opposite give-away budget' is scarcely an adequate rendering of it. What there is here is an illusion of balance, whereby reports are included from what appear as different sides. But the reported views have a totally different status, legitimacy and meaning in the text. In a very real way, only one set of statements makes 'sense' in that we are systematically given the information necessary to understand the explanations and policies which they represent.

Rationality and hard 'realism' are thus presented as being the prerogative of those who are in favour of wage restraint and of allowing unemployment to rise. The bitter attacks of those who were opposed to this were at times reported on the news, but they remained at the level of emotional appeals against the apparently 'inevitable', since the logic and rationale of these alternative viewpoints were substantially absent. The difference in the manner in which the two sides were made to appear was clearly summarised in a B.B.C. bulletin on the day after the budget. The item began,

> The Chancellor had to face his own Parliamentary colleagues today with explanations about his budget which, as he had admitted yesterday, could increase both the cost of living and unemployment. One of our Westminster staff said criticisms and praise were evenly matched. *Right wingers said the budget was realistic, left wingers said it wasn't socialist.* (B.B.C. 1 2100 16 April 1975)

Yet throughout the period of our study, there were alternative views available both of the nature of the economic crisis and of how it might be resolved. One of the key premises of those who were outrightly opposed to the policy of lowering wages and cutting public expenditure, was that the economic crisis had not been caused by working people and that therefore they should not be made to pay for it. To understand this point of view, it would be necessary to have an alternative view of what had caused inflation and economic decline. As we have already indicated, one crucial dimension to this alternative view was the failure of many capitalist firms over a long period to engage in adequate investment in new plant and in advanced technology. The effect of this had been to make a large section of British industry inefficient relative to its foreign competitors. The reason for this is simply that private investment is undertaken for profit and money is invested where it will receive the highest return. This is not necessarily in productive industry. One effect of this in recent years has been that huge sums of investment capital were moved away from industrial production into other activities such as speculation in land, property and food. The process by which this occurred was summarised in an editorial in the *Investors' Chronicle*. Here it was argued that,

> In the summer of 1973, the government was allowing the amount of money for use in the country to expand rapidly in the hope that industry would use it to invest in new plant to produce more goods and earn more foreign exchange by exporting.

It did not work out that way, because industry was not confident that it could sell enough goods profitably enough to cover the money for new plant. So the extra money being pumped into the economy found other uses.

At first some of it found its way into buying shares where it helped to force prices up. More important, vast amounts of money were being lent by the banking system to buy property. Since property is in limited supply, the main effect was to force prices sky high. (*Investors' Chronicle* 11 September 1974)

It was partly because of the failure of private investment to produce growth and stability in the economy that many members of the Labour Party and the trade unions were demanding that investment be organised and controlled by the Government. This might have included, for example, the nationalisation of insurance companies which were key sources of investment and the expansion of publicly-owned industries. The understanding of factors such as the decline in investment is thus crucial for those explanations of the economy which do not focus merely on 'excessive wages' as the source of all problems.

This is of great importance in analysing the presentation of ideas in the television news. For our argument so far has been that the dominance of a specific way of understanding the world will crucially affect the manner in which alternative ideas appear. We have said that there are obvious *numerical* differences between references to the two themes of wages and investment as economic problems. However, we are also arguing that because the news is produced from within a limited view, its content is organised in such a way that coherence and order is given to only one set of explanations and policies. The logic of one group of explanations is built into the text, from the premise that wage increases have caused inflation and crisis to the conclusion that wage restraint and higher taxation are therefore necessary. This is shown very clearly in the following example from the B.B.C. 2 *News Review*, of the week after the budget of April 1975.

Now home, and as you know this week there's been a lot of

heavy news on the country's economic front. Two figures from the week give the real story. Everything else in one way or another is reaction to those figures. One: prices rose in the last twelve months by the biggest ever increase, 21 per cent. Two: wages rose in the last twelve months by a far greater figure, 32 per cent. The Chancellor for one regards that extra 11 per cent on wages as the main cause of inflation. His answer as we saw in the budget on Tuesday, is to take the extra money away in taxes. (B.B.C. 2 1815 20 April 1975)

A remarkable synthesis is thus made between a narrow and restricted economic explanation and the political policies which apparently flow from it. By comparison, when references to the decline in investment did appear, there was no sense in which this problem was related to a whole way of understanding the nature of the economy and how its problems might be solved. In general this decline was treated rather as a 'natural' and unavoidable disaster. For example, the following report appeared on I.T.N. in January 1975:

Bad economic news for the Government on two fronts today – investment by companies is now expected to be as much as 10 per cent down this year compared with 1974 and unemployment is still accelerating upwards. The investment forecast comes from a survey of firms' intentions published by the Department of Trades and Industry. The Department says the money that firms spend on new plant and equipment is expected to be between 7 per cent and 10 per cent down this year. That compares to the original forecast which showed it would in fact rise slightly. And today's survey says that the forecast for next year is that investment will be even lower. On unemployment there haven't been any Government figures for two months because of an internal staffing dispute. However, Sir Denis Barnes, Chairman of the Manpower Services Commission, warns that the forecast of higher unemployment appears to be coming true. He said more firms will sooner or later be forced into announcing redundancies. (I.T.N. 1750 21 January 1975)

The only causal link that appears to be made here is

between investment and unemployment. There is no explanation of why investment is declining or that this decline was part of a long process which might explain the nature of the economic crisis. Perhaps more significant, the figures are not related to contemporary political policies. For example, the Industry Bill which was designed to increase public investment and to expand public ownership was to be introduced into the Commons by Mr Anthony Wedgwood Benn ten days after these figures appeared. There is no sense in which the inclusion of such fragmented references to the decline of investment could be compared with the consistent monitoring of wages and prices figures and the use of these by the media to underline political policies. While the figures for investment were reported almost in a vacuum, those for wages and prices were consistently used to emphasise the view that wage increases were the central problem, and were thus linked to the policies of wage restraint and to the harsh deflation of the budget. It must be said in addition that the figures on the relation between wages and prices were very ambiguous at this time and there is considerable evidence to suggest that real wages were in fact falling through the period of our sample. None the less the television news on both channels consistently concluded that wages were 'soaring' ahead of prices. In the following example from B.B.C. news of April 1975, this view is linked to a specific political position,

> After Mr Healey's tough budget warning about recent pay rises being too big, Government figures have disclosed that wage rates have jumped up nearly a third in the past year and that's a record. The increase between February and March alone was close on 4 per cent, the second highest monthly rise ever. Here's our industrial correspondent, Ian Ross.

> Ian Ross: Well these figures rub in Mr Healey's warnings about wage-led inflation and pay rises well in excess of the cost of living – and they reveal a widening disparity between pay and prices. (B.B.C. 1 2100 16 April 1975)

One factor in the consistent conclusion on the news that wage rises were 'well in excess' of prices was that the official figures were frequently given without important qualifications which might point to different conclusions. These included at the very minimum the need to allow for tax and other deductions, to indicate the 'real' value of wage increases. In the case of I.T.N., out of a total of eleven occasions during the period of our sample in which the wage/price figures were reported, six of these made no reference to where real wages might have been in relation to prices, but gave only the gross figures for apparent wage increases. For the B.B.C. (taking both B.B.C. 1 and B.B.C. 2 together) the gross figures were given without reference to real wages in seventeen bulletins out of a total of twenty during the same period. The view that wage increases are the central economic problem was thus underlined and developed in the organisation of the news coverage. By comparison the failure of the system of private investment was treated rather as an unavoidable disaster, and remained substantially unexplored. On only three occasions in this whole period of four months was a direct link made between investment, the economic crisis and inflation. These were all in small fragmented reports of the views of Mr Anthony Wedgwood Benn. In January 1975 he was quoted as follows,

> The Industry Secretary, Mr Benn, today gave his explanation for the country's industrial failure, for which he said working people had become the most popular scapegoats. The real cause was lack of investment and he said inflation was the result of overpriced goods produced with outdated equipment by underpaid workers. (B.B.C. 1 2200 25 January 1975)

We have shown how 'wage–inflation' as a theme in the analysis of economic crisis massively outnumbered alternative explanations. This was at a time when the industrial correspondent of I.T.N. had noted that 'Since the war, Britain's over-riding problem, almost universally agreed, has been a failure to invest adequately' (I.T.N. 2200 21 January 1975, quoted above). In total, the references to wages as a problem and wage restraint as a solution numbered 383 in the four-month period. By comparison, the number of references to the decline of investment as a problem and the need to increase it as a solution, totalled only eighty-nine. This figure actually over-emphasises the role of investment and the failure of private industry as explanations in the news. References to these, when they came, occurred usually in a fragmented and disparate fashion, and were very rarely part of a coherent alternative view of the economy and the nature of its problems. There was no regular and systematic analysis on the news of the failure of private industry or of what had happened to the system of private investment. It was merely acknowledged that there was a 'problem' with it. By comparison, the activities of trade unions were consistently scrutinised and linked to the failure of the economy. Individual wage claims were systematically and critically evaluated. For example, in the following interview with the General Secretary of ASLEF, the I.T.N. newscaster states,

> Can we look at your claim you've already got in; you see, I mean, you said to one of my colleagues not long ago on this programme that this claim was likely then – this was in February – to be in the range of 25 per cent to 30 per cent; now, you see, that is already between 5 per cent and 10 per cent more than the rise in prices *and it's just this excessive demand above the price rise that Mr Healey was saying was endangering our whole national economy.* (I.T.N. 1300 16 April 1975)

The news thus established the context within which the activities of trade unionists may be judged as unreasonable and dangerous. In the following example from B.B.C. news of February 1975, the miners' pay negotiations are juxtaposed with Mr Healey's view of the economy and of what must be done in it:

> The Chancellor of the Exchequer, Mr Healey, has warned again of excessive wage increases as the miners start negotiating on their claim for up to 43 per cent. Mr Healey said in London tonight that Britain could be bankrupt if the national wage bill were too high this year – but it needn't happen if the workers stuck strictly to the Social Contract. During the day the Coal Board twice increased their offer to the miners, mainly to the benefit of those working un-

derground. They are now prepared to pay between 25 and 30 per cent more. Here's our industrial correspondent, Ian Ross.

Ian Ross: What the Coal Board is now offering the miners is certainly not the strict interpretation of the Social Contract that Mr Healey is insisting on. (B.B.C. 1 2100 11 February 1975)

The overall emphasis given to Healey's views throughout news reports of the period provides the basis for a *direct embracing* by the news of a political position. 'Reason' and 'rationality' thus become the qualities only of those who fall in exactly with the partial view of the news producers. This is made quite clear in the following exchange between a trade unionist from the National Union of Bank Employees and an I.T.N. presenter:

Interviewee: Our job as a trade union is to maintain the purchasing power of our members' salaries and that's all we're trying to do with the pay claim that we've now formulated.

I.T.N. presenter: But as reasonable men and responsible citizens can you say that's all you are trying to do and all you are interested in when you hear warnings from the Chancellor to the effect that increases of this sort are going to wreck the national economy? (I.T.N. 1300 24 February 1975)

The problems of an economic system are thus reduced to the irresponsible actions of trade unionists. In real terms, the wages of British workers had not increased significantly for four years prior to our study, and they lagged well behind the wages paid in Europe and the United States by Britain's competitors. Throughout the period of our study real wages for the mass of Britain's working population, were in fact declining. *The Times* reported in August 1975 that average earnings in the first half of the year rose by 6.1 per cent, yet,

Retail prices over the same half year, rose by 17.3 per cent, implying a drop in the value of the average pay packet of nearly 10 per cent. (*The Times* 21 August 1975)

The investment crisis of private capital and the consequent low productivity of British industry was at the heart of the economic problem. As the *Economist* had noted as early as 1972,

> After all, it has been Britain's failure of productivity rather than wages that has made us more inflation-prone than other countries. (The *Economist*, 4 November 1972)

Yet on the television news, in the period of our study, 'high' wage awards were consistently singled out as the source of the economic problem. This is not an argument merely about differences of opinion on economic theories. The laying of the blame for the failure of Britain's economy at the door of the trade unions was a central part of the political policies which made the mass of population pay for the economic crisis – through lower wages, higher taxes and ultimately cuts in Government spending and unemployment. The views of those who disagreed with this and who offered alternative approaches were down-graded and under-represented in the news coverage. This is in stark comparison with the careful explanation and heavy emphasis given to the dominant analysis which was that of Mr Healey, the Treasury and the CBI.

The content of news and the manner in which it is organised thus embodies a specific way of understanding the social and industrial world. In essence our case is that the numerical repetition of certain themes and explanations together with the embracing and underlining of them by media journalists are parts of a general process by which the news is produced from within this limited and partial world view. This is reflected in the choice of material, the themes that are emphasised, the links that are made between these, and the final conclusions that are drawn. At times, as we have shown, fragments of alternative information appear which could be linked, developed and emphasised to produce a quite different view of the social world and of what moves it. It is a measure of the pervasiveness of the dominant explanations and politics of the news that this was never done in the whole period of our study.

Our analysis thus goes beyond saying merely that the television news 'favours' certain individuals or institutions by giving them more time or status. The problem is deeper than this. In the end it relates to the picture of society that television news consistently constructs. This at its most damaging amounts to laying the blame for the problems of an economy based on private interest at the door of the workforce.

2

May the First, 1973 – a Day of Predictable Madness

JOCK YOUNG
Principal Lecturer in Sociology, Middlesex Polytechnic
J. BROOKE CRUTCHLEY
Senior Lecturer in Sociology, Middlesex Polytechnic

You'll have to bulldoze your way through in business; be tough and be extra energetic in forcing the pace. Good day for those working at the bench, those handling machinery – or dealing in it or metals. Whatever your work, your output should be that much greater than usual.
Horoscope for May Day, *Evening Standard* (30 April 1973).

May the first – for those who believe in astrology – was obviously not a day to waste on demonstrations. Even 1 May 1973, which saw the largest trade union demonstrations of recent years, against the Conservative Party's Industrial Relations Act, an act which was designed to 'control' trade unionism. Gazing into their crystal balls in the weeks before May Day, media spokesmen failed to relate these threatened protests to incipient changes in consciousness amongst British trade unionists. James Halloran and his co-workers concluded in regard to liberal protest movements that accounts in the media are 'largely isolated from antecedent conditions, conveying little understanding of either root causes or aims; and that the whole interpretation will convey a generally negative impression' (Halloran *et al.*, *Demonstrations and Communications*, Penguin, 1970, p. 315). An analysis of media coverage of May Day 1973 indicates this conclusion can be generalised to treatment by Press, radio and television of industrial affairs.

Any event taken out of its proper context is infinitely interpretable. Just as a glass of beer can be half full to an optimist and half empty to his pessimistic comrade, a strike can be a pitiful failure from one perspective yet a portent of a burgeoning class consciousness to another. Our aim is to indicate how the mass media coverage was not so much distorted in detail – although a host of minor inaccuracies occurred – but represented out of context a limited and specious model of society.

The Industrial Relations Act of 1972 can be viewed from two entirely opposing perspectives. In terms of consensus politics it was a triumph of reason. The State, representing the national interest of the majority, would be able to intervene in labour disputes – economic conflicts would be subsumed and adjudicated under the rule of law. By contrast, from a class perspective the Act was a blatant ruling-class attempt at union bashing and a direct weakening of the powers of working-class organisations. In consensus terms then, resistance to the Act was sheer irrationality which would lead to social anarchy, but from the point of view of the class struggle, resistance was an eminently rational defence against a singularly oppressive piece of legislation. It is our contention that the world view of the mass media depicted the May Day strike against the Act entirely in consensual terms and that this was achieved from a standpoint of historical myopia.

Between 1 July 1970 – two weeks after the Conservative Party were returned to power – and 31 March 1973, 45.6 million working days were lost in industrial stoppages. In 1972 the number of working days lost (23.9 million) was the highest since 1926. Approximately the same number of days were lost in industrial disputes in 1972 as during the whole period of the 1964–70 Labour Government. Class conflict was on the upsurge. The sporadic walk-outs of the years of affluence were being replaced by sustained trials of strength between trade unionists and government. In a review of the trend of strikes Michael Silver came to the following conclusion:

> ... the situation now is that the niggly unofficial strikes which seemed to be bringing Britain to the verge of

economic destruction only five years ago are lessening in significance because of the massive and lengthy confrontations in coal and cars, and by dockers, dustmen and train drivers, that have become part of the industrial scene of the 1970s. ('Recent British Strike Trends', *British Journal of Industrial Relations*, March 1973)

1972 was a highpoint in working-class struggle. Massive solidarity had obtained the release of three London dockers' leaders from Pentonville Prison. The A.U.E.W. simply refused to pay fines imposed by the Industrial Relations Court. Above all, the miners made a wage claim which was in excess of the government's pay limits and, with widespread support, this eventually forced the government to back down.

By February 1973, as discontent crystallised around the government's freeze on wages, the situation seemed critical to many on both left and right. Three-quarters of a million gasmen, hospital workers, engine drivers, civil servants, teachers and car workers were threatening strike action. A re-run of the 1972 miner's strike appeared to be likely and the imminent outbreak of overt class warfare became a distinct possibility. The bellicose mood of the *Economist*'s leading editorial in late February reflects this fear from the viewpoint of the beleaguered ruling class. The nation was solemnly warned on 24 February that 'next week will be a very crucial one in Britain. This is the time for each individual to decide for himself how to act.'

The only excuse any striker can plead is that other trade unions have already robbed more than they can from the old and the workless . . . and that they must be allowed their turn in the muggers' queue . . . [furthermore] whether they realise it or not, all who obey a strike call next week will be much more akin to those who go mugging for fun or through mindlessness than those who do so for gain.

It was in this atmosphere that the T.U.C. formed a Special Conference for a national campaign of protest (5 March). At the beginning of spring, after a coal strike had been averted and things had returned to 'normal', a more sober appraisal prevailed in the columns of the *Economist*. They were now of the opinion that the government had been able to 'ambush the weak stragglers of last year's wage claim army' (*Economist* 24 March, p. 73). The hospital workers, London teachers and civil servants were always likely to lose 'because they had no real industrial power'.

In the changed circumstances certain half-hearted sections of the trade union movement became more so and the headlines reporting Vic Feather's 'resentful and reluctant acquiescence in Phase Two of the pay policy' completed the apparent defusion of the industrial crisis. Although many union members denounced such a position as defeatist and many others merely registered that a temporary setback had occurred, the notion of trade union acquiescence and even acceptance of government policy became the dominant media theme. Consequently the historic context of the May Day demonstration was systematically obscured by the media in their restricted and one-sided interpretation of affairs. But the size and significance of an event cannot be judged outside of its history. May Day should not be seen in the short-term perspective of union setbacks and the half-hearted militancy of many union leaders. Rather it must be perceived in the long-term perspective of the rarity of national political strikes involving many unions and in the context of the mounting industrial tension. Only in such a setting can we talk of events being predictable or surprising or failures. But because neither reflection on the recent past nor speculation on the immediate future informed media coverage of May Day 1973, they were unable to interpret its social significance.

In attempting a structured analysis of media coverage of industrial conflict we examined the national press from March to early May and recorded radio and television coverage on 1 May, the day the papers did not appear. This account represents a review of this research.

In terms of a consensus view, action against the Act was a violation of the rationality of the majority of citizens. From this premise one could predict that its motivation was an act of irrationality and furthermore, that only a small minority would support the strike call. Thus the framework of analysis was already cast before the event. May the first would be a day of predictable madness.

During the run up to the day attempts were made to show the demonstration was irrelevant. The *Economist* sought to resuscitate bygone days by arguing 'YOU'VE NEVER HAD IT BETTER' (7 April) and thought with a little bit of 'luck' we (not Mr Health alone) would see it through (24 March). This theme asserted that government policies were either already working or were on the brink of working. All that was needed was a bit of public relations to secure the innate goodwill of the British public 'What really matters now is that most trade unionists have accepted as fair the £1 – plus 4% limit' (*Daily Mail* 30 April). 'The revolution has already taken place – in the general levelling up of living standards' (*Daily Express* 30 April).

Given that everything in the garden is rosy why then should anyone want to strike? The answer was simple: 'MAY DAY MADNESS' was a leader headline in four papers (*Sun, Sunday Express, News of the World, Evening News*). Yet compared with the good old affluent days, today's world is clearly out of joint. Media spokesmen see this dislocation not in the protracted international currency crisis or in rising world food prices but in the star-struck militants who devilishly lead common folk astray. Thus Robert Robinson on the early morning *Today* radio programme (7 a.m.) described the forthcoming events of the day as 'saturnine' and the *Observer* (29 April) talked of a 'Red Gesture'.

The *Daily Express* appraised the May events as the 'last spasm of old fashioned industrial warfare', an 'irrelevant hiccup of anger by the Labour Movement' (30 April). The only sane activity was 'to try not to think about it' in the words of a no-nonsense traffic warden interviewed on the *World at One* radio programme. Let's 'forget this sad irrelevance' for 'it's an embarrassment all round' (*Daily Mail* 30 April) and 'get this silly day over with and get back to serious work' (*Evening News* 30 April), for 'no seasoned union leader can regard the May Day stoppages as anything but a footling gesture which at best became necessary by an accident of union politics' (*The Times* 28 April). The 'serious work' was obviously the negotiations between government and unions. These were secretly initiated at the end of April and revealed by the *Mirror* in a front page scoop on 29 April. But first the hot-heads had to have their fling.

The predictable consequence of madness is impotency. Because 'most people believe that the May Day strike is a waste of time' (*Evening News* 30 April); it is 'the strike nobody wants' and 'only a relative handful of trade unions will join' (*Daily Mail* 30 April) because 'many workers feel the anti-government protest is now pointless (*Daily Telegraph* 30 April). The whole exercise was envisaged as an irrational lashing out at society at large, a 'token gesture of temporary bloody-mindedness' where 'so many will have to put up with so much inconvenience and loss' (*Sunday Telegraph* 29 April). The militants will not accept that 'in a complicated society we cannot live by tribal rules which classify employees as Us and employers as Them' for management 'are acting as trustees for the whole company . . . in which everyone's interests are involved' (*Daily Express* 30 April).

On the day itself, with Fleet Street silent, the May Day events were only once accorded more than third rank importance. On the I.T.N. *News at Ten* the day of protest and stoppage featured as their second main news item. The feature that invariably pushed the strike news into third place was the second rank importance awarded to the E.E.C. farm price review in Luxembourg. Almost without exception reportage of this diplomatic battle was not related – either directly or indirectly – to the reiterated demand of interviewed trade unionists for a freeze on food prices. Saturation coverage throughout the day of Nixon's Watergate escapade ensured foreign news received premiere attention throughout the day.

Visual presentation of the day's events were dominated by transport news. A train from Enfield that *did* run. A Sergeant Major acting as traffic warden in Horse Guards Parade. An aerial view of a jam-packed roundabout. While all emphasised the mysterious ubiquity of the strike none departed from the basic formula of the day's happenings as an irrational non-event. Regional coverage of absenteeism and demonstrations resembled the liturgy of the football results although we were always in doubt which league the data referred to. No attempt was made to relate 'the biggest demonstration in Birmingham in living memory' to the widespread prosperity and 'affluent' Conservative voting in that region a few elections ago. Everything was taken for granted.

Robert Dougal told us on the B.B.C. *Nine o'clock News* that things had 'gone off largely as expected' as we watched Scotland Yard keeping a vigilant eye on video screens monitoring accident blackspots. A potential threat to the social order was reduced to the level of such natural media laws as traffic jams on Bank Holidays.

A more obvious bias came from interviewer style. There are two variants. In one model spokesmen of contrasting persuasion are precipitated into verbal combat stage-managed and effectively censored by a consensual compere. Alternatively, a solo militant celebrity is interviewed by a belligerent interviewer who absurdly overstates the reactionary viewpoint. Both formats were in evidence on both channels during the monitored programmes. Obviously our brief study cannot say anything conclusive about trends. However with the announcement of secret talks between top union leaders and the government a couple of days after May Day a more beguiling tone of questioning could be detected on the part of the professional interviewers. Consensual style – unlike consensual analysis – is not an invariant property of the make-up of media men.

The reappearance of the papers was accompanied by a post-mortem. Beforehand, Fleet Street had concentrated on opinion to the detriment of factual information. To some extent this contrasts with the typical stance by all radio and telecasts.

The morning after, the papers certainly signalled loudly the success of their prediction. 'WHAT A FLOP' asserted the headline in the *Sun*. All other papers followed suit, even though the numbers on strike were 60 per cent above the predicted one million which had become standard currency in Fleet Street and despite the occurrence of massive nationwide demonstrations, the plans for which the press had almost completely omitted to mention prior to the event. In the only front page comment the *Daily Mail* proclaimed it was 'work as usual for May Day Millions'. The *Daily Telegraph* was of the opinion it was 'the most futile gesture in the history of British

Trade Unionism', for as their headline emphasised 'MILLIONS IGNORE T.U.C. DAY OF PROTEST'. Such moralising was, however, more eye-catching than cerebral. A glaring contradiction could be detected between the alleged futility of the event and the extent of its consequences.

The *Sun*'s headlined verdict 'What a Flop' was followed by an extensive catalogue of industrial paralysis. 'Railways were shut almost completely. Car workers shut most of the four big firms. Miners closed 113 collieries. Dockers stopped work at Hull, Liverpool, Manchester and Bristol. Engineering firms were badly hit. No national newspapers were published.' Even punters were hit! Similarly the *Daily Mail* noted that 'only in the car plants did the militants score a big success' while apologising for not appearing the previous day – in common with all the other national papers.

This contradiction was partially solved by the expediency adopted by the *Daily Mirror* of placing successes and failures in binary opposition down one whole page. Separating these balanced extremes was a long slender picture of the London march filling the whole length of Oxford Street. The *Financial Times* solved the problem with ease by keeping a careful ambivalence on its front page whilst listing with grim thoroughness the economic bite of the strike on its back page. In such a fashion the palpable failure of the model used by the media was shored up against the devastations of empirical reality. Thus on the radio the *World at One* interviewer listed the dire effects of the strike and then asked just 'how irrelevant is this May Day protest?'. It took Vic Feather – who appeared on radio and both television channels at some point during the evening although he had not himself participated in any march or meeting – to puncture such *non sequiturs*: 'When people don't see eye to eye with what we do they say it's irrelevant . . . I would have thought if something was a futile gesture they would not get so upset about it' (5 p.m. radio interview).

Both the anticipation of May Day and depiction of the events themselves were structured in terms of an irrelevant strike that nobody wanted – an absurd non-event. The predictions from the model evolved in the month prior to the event were almost by definition verified. Thus ironically a favourite phrase on the prompt sheets of every media commentator was 'it's all so predictable'. Presumably only a total general strike or a revolutionary insurrection could have injected any element of surprise into the model.

All of this holds together with a thin and desperate logic. To sociologists it has the instantly recognisable features of a consensus model of society where all members are supposed to have common values and interests and any deviancy is seen as accidental, irrational or madness. It was around such a model that news was selected or systematically ignored if it did not fit.

The media then select from the truth: it is not a question of simple distortion. They take up parts of reality (for example the T.U.C. *was* half-hearted) and give them exclusive coverage omitting all other shades of opinions. Further, they place truths (for example the numbers on strike *were* less than two million) and interpret them outside of an appropriate historical context. All this represents an implicit and largely unconscious defence of the *status quo*. Lord Goodman, Chairman of the Newspapers Proprietors' Association, blithely maintained on the B.B.C. *Midweek* programme (B.B.C. 1 May, 11 p.m.) that a total spectrum of opinion is represented in the British Press. He attacked the newspaper unions in particular for impeding the freedom of the Press. Yet, in this area at least, there was no such spectrum; there was a unanimity of opinion which by virtue of its monolithic nature might well take on the appearance of a taken-for-granted reality to certain segments of the population. Because of this, what was, in fact, a sizeable manifestation of political class conflict rare in British history in terms of both scale and range of support, became in image, as represented in the media, a predictable act of May Day Madness.

Thus an event, which was part of a sustained struggle against the Act which led up to the political destruction of the Heath Government in 1974 in the second confrontation with the miners, was reported as a solitary act of irrationality. This is the character of the 'free' media.

3

Press and Prejudice

FRANCIS BECKETT

Formerly Press Officer, National Union of Students

On 12 October 1972 Her Royal Highness Queen Elizabeth II visited Stirling University. Conflicting reports on precisely what happened that day need not concern us here. But here are some facts about that day on which all authorities and witnesses seem to agree.

1. At no time was the Queen in any physical danger whatsoever. ('The Government is satisfied that the Queen was not in danger from student demonstrators at Stirling University last week, Mr Carr, Home Secretary, said last night in a Commons written answer' – small news item at the bottom of an inside page of the *Sunday Telegraph*, 21 October 1972.)

2. At no time was any physical violence against the Queen intended, attempted, discussed, threatened or in any way likely.

3. The Queen herself was not frightened or intimidated. ('The Queen was seemingly unperturbed' – *The Times*. 'Throughout it all the Queen remained smiling and unruffled' – *Daily Telegraph*. 'All through yesterday's riotous scenes the Queen kept her smile' – *Sun*. 'The Queen was not unduly concerned for her safety' – a Buckingham Palace spokesman quoted in the *Sun*. 'The Queen kept cool and smiling' – *Daily Mail*. 'The Queen was neither disturbed nor distressed by the demonstration' – *Guardian*. 'The Queen was smiling and seemingly unruffled' – *Yorkshire Post*. 'Still she smiled' – *Daily Express*. All the above quotations appeared on 13 October, the day after the demonstration.)

A news judgement was, however, made: a professional judgement that this was the most important, significant or interesting event to have happened the previous day. Stirling was the main front page story in both London evening papers on 12 October and every national daily on the morning of 13 October. We have heard a good deal about the value of having a diverse press. On this occasion, as on many others, there was no diversity, no breaking of ranks: every news editor in London made the same decision. The four national popular newspapers looked like this:

Daily Mail

Front page lead:

'QUEEN COURAGEOUS – Drunk students hurl insults at Royal visitor'

Front page second lead:

'SCUM says police chief'

Continuation page 2:

'The Queen faces jeering mob'

Daily Express

Front page lead:

'Drunken students chant obscene songs as a guarding hand protects her from jostling crowd'

'The obscene and beery breath of student violence came frighteningly close to the Queen yesterday at Stirling University'

(And three photographs.)

'Photonews', inside page:

'Smiling through regally'

'Still she smiled ... around her students mocked with jeering toasts as they swigged at bottles of beer and cheap wine'

'Only feet away from her, fists flailed. Foul-mouthed university louts yelled obscenities ...'

Another inside page headline:

'A queenly lesson in calm and composure for university louts ... as supposedly educated youngsters they're a disgrace, says police chief'

Sun

Front page lead:

'STUDENT MOB INSULTS THE QUEEN

A howling mob of drunken students hurled insults at the Queen yesterday'

Daily Mirror

Front page lead:

'DRUNKEN STUDENTS MOB THE QUEEN

Royal party jeered by wine-swigging rowdies

The Queen was surrounded by a frightening mob of drunken students who swore and chanted obscenities yesterday . . .'

Observe:

1. The continual emphasis on 'student mob'.
2. The fact that the *Daily Express* thought that it made things worse that the wine was cheap – it became a rude adjective to put in the lead paragraph. What would the *Express* have said about student grants had the wine been the sort that *Express* editors drink?
3. The emphasis throughout on drunkenness – which appeared in all reports except those in the *Guardian, The Times* and *Morning Star*, newspapers which do occasionally let the facts interfere with the news. Not the slightest evidence for drunkenness has ever been produced.

It is well worth dwelling on this question of the sobriety or otherwise of the students for a moment. Every newspaper carried the most violent photograph it could find from the whole incident the following day. Over the next few months that photograph became significant, worth further reproduction in endless flashbacks, analyses and what have you, even though on 13 October it had appeared on almost everyone's front page. It shows a student taking a drink from a wine bottle within a few yards of the Queen.

Now the Queen – 'not unduly worried' (Buckingham Palace spokesman) and 'laughing and having enjoyed herself immensely' (Sir Derek Lang, University Secretary) – left the same day and probably forgot the incident unless she is an avid reader of the popular Press.

Not so the other person in the photograph – tracked down by the Press the following day and identified as thirty-four year old student Jack Mackie, married with three children. 'I did not insult her. I was not drunk. All I said to the Queen was "Slainte Mhath", a Gaelic toast', he told the newspapers. And that, from all the evidence, is entirely true.

Mr Mackie is worth mentioning because over the next few months he was thrown out of his lodgings with his wife and three children: beaten when walking around the town and spat on and insulted in bars and cafes. None of these incidents were reported in the newspapers which had caused them. The thing became a running story. Over the next few months every trivial development in Stirling University internal politics was thought to be of absorbing interest to the readers of every national newspaper in the land. Poor Mr Mackie's wine bottle – the most expensive bottle of 'cheap wine' he ever bought – was trotted out in endless flashbacks lest anyone had forgotten. Stirling University Students' Union President Linda Quinn's face became, fleetingly, as well known as the Prime Minister's. It was not until 12 February 1973 – four months later – that the *Guardian* was in a position to squeeze what looked like the last column inch the 'Stirling affair' was worth in a national newspaper. A *Guardian* leader headed 'A fresh start at Stirling' noted that 'Apart from brief paragraphs and letters, the affairs of Stirling University have almost disappeared from non-Scottish newspapers . . .' Almost, but not quite. There was a brief, unpleasant revival of the whole affair when Stirling's Principal, Dr Tom Cottrell, died later the same year. More dreary flashbacks, and the subtly hinted question: had Cottrell been driven to his death by 'the obscene and beery breath of student violence'? Now, why did all this happen? What was the reason for the obsessive interest in the 'Stirling affair'?

The mechanics are simple. Every national newspaper made the same snap news judgement on 12 October: this was a big story, a very big story indeed, the biggest. The rest followed inevitably. The Press had committed itself to following up the story. The readers demanded it. There was no turning back. If

you begin to read a fairy tale to a child and decide half way through that it's boring and another would be better, the child will not let you change stories: it wants to know how this one is going to end. So with Stirling. It would have been useless for the Press to decide, say in November, that maybe they had made a mistake on 12 October, maybe in the long term the war in Vietnam was going to matter more. The die was cast.

And after the Press came the pundits. Every press officer and every publicity-conscious politician knows that, to get your comments in the newspapers, you have to be ready to react to the headlines of the day, not the things which are happening which you think are important. And if enough pundits weren't commenting, diligent journalists spent hours chasing them for a quote. Would the N.U.S. make a statement? No, the N.U.S. would not make a statement. Such was the fever that one got headlines even for NOT making a statement.

Lord Annan thought it was disgusting. A brace of Tory M.P.s thought it showed that student grants were too high. Mr Norman St John Stevas thought it was disgraceful. The Committee of Vice Chancellors were shocked. Mr Bernard Levin was furious. Lord Nugent of Guildford found it 'difficult to understand how anyone in this country could be offensive to a woman, let alone the Queen'. Mr John Bigg-Davidson said something but I can't remember what it was. Everyone who thought he was someone, or could be made to look like someone for a day, got his name in the papers.

Now, why? The Press long ago gave up giving front page treatment to student demonstrations. Even an occupation of a university administration building only merits a few obscure paragraphs these days. As for the Queen, her daily doings, what she is opening today, where she planted a tree yesterday and what statue she is going to unveil tomorrow – news editors yawn when it's even mentioned. But the combination proved irresistible.

Stirling may not have been either important or interesting, but it was NEWS. And the essential reason that it was news was not in any way intrinsic to the event itself. The reason it was news was the tautological reason that it appeared in the newspapers. That, and nothing else about the incident, gave it the status of the principal saloon-bar discussion topic for months, one on which the Secretary of State for Education, and even the Prime Minister, was asked to say something. And that is the power, the terrible power, that is vested in the newspaper industry. When newspapers try to tell people what to think about, they are generally successful. They are successful because newspapers are one of our most important means of hearing about what is going on in the world. We trust their news judgement, often without even thinking about it. And so, if Stirling is the major news item in every national newspaper one day, and an important running story for months afterwards, then Stirling matters.

Newspapers, then, have one great power: the power to decide what the issues are. But they have another great power: the power of news presentation. If you look back for a moment to our catalogue of 13 October headlines about Stirling, you will find that there was not only unanimity of purpose about the news value of the event: there was also a snap value–judgement. No amount of thoughtful features in heavy newspapers over the next few months cancelled that judgement, expressed in the heaviest possible type in all the most prominent places. The students were drunk, they were louts, they were scum; their breath was obscene and beery, they were violent and foul-mouthed, they were a mob, they were wine-swigging rowdies. In other words, the newspapers had expressed value-judgement in news coverage. They had expressed that judgement, not by saying editorially that they, the newspapers, disapproved of the students' action, but by word selection. Two words can have exactly the same objective meaning, and a totally different emotive effect. Thus students at Stirling didn't shout, they howled; they didn't drink wine, they swigged it; there wasn't a group of them, there was a mob; they didn't sing songs, they chanted them; and don't forget that the wine was cheap. You had to read the *Guardian* to find that 'the protest was against the unnecessary expense of the visit' and the *Morning Star* to discover that 'Students' Association President Linda Quinn said yesterday that student welfare had been ignored while the authorities made a fuss about the visit'.

The Stirling affair showed the capacity and willingness of newspapers to build up a relatively small incident into a *cause célèbre*, and to use it to discredit people. In the case of Stirling, students as students were by implication discredited. That is the power of the Press. But how far is the Press prepared to use that power? Paul Hoch, with two years at the London School of Economics behind him, wrote in 1974:

> In the past few years newspapers have been full of story after story of revolutionary students infringing the so-called rights of free speech of establishment politicians and generals. Ironically the publishers and commentators screaming loudest about these heinous crimes are precisely the people who ensure that these abused politicians have roughly a thousand times as much access to the official organs of public opinion as the people abusing them . . . Of course, anyone is free to start a newspaper – just as anyone is free to start a chain of luxury hotels. All you need is a few millions and the sort of opinions that won't antagonise any large block of distributors or advertisers. (Paul Hoch, *The Newspaper Game*, Calder and Boyars, 1974)

While Hoch was writing, N.U.S. officials were meeting a man called Jurij Sayamov, one of the leaders of the Student Council of the U.S.S.R., who came to England for the press conference which launched the N.U.S. campaign on Northern Ireland. What did Jurij think about our free Press when he left the next day? He had heard leaders describe their campaign for a restoration of civil rights in Northern Ireland. When asked, he had said yes, he agreed with them. He had then gone sightseeing, had a couple of drinks, gone to bed and woken up in time for his plane, his work in England done.

He was brought the *Daily Express*, where he read the headline:

RED
JURIJ
LEADS
DRIVE
TO AID
THE IRA

Just to spell it out: Jurij was leading nothing. There was no drive to aid the I.R.A. Did Jurij feel deprived, back in Moscow, that his country did not have the blessing of a free Press?

Two years had elapsed since Stirling, and there had been a truce. After the 'obscene and beery breath of students' violence' at Stirling, there was a backlash against students as a whole. The trouble with that, from a newspaper's point of view, is that there are over half a million students. That means about a million parents, maybe the same number of non-student brothers, sisters and friends – not far short of three million people, all of whom know that students aren't like that. Three million people is a sizeable section of the population for even a national newspaper to take on.

The war was called off. Throughout 1973 the *Daily Express*'s Education Correspondent Bruce Kemble was allowed to report, as fully and fairly as anything is reported in the *Express*, on the student grants campaign. He was even allowed to write features sympathetic to better student grants, to quote the N.U.S., and to collaborate with the N.U.S. in finding case histories which showed hardship resulting from the existing grants system. Thus on 6 February 1973 we read about

THE STRUGGLING STUDENT
Linda Vaughan whose widowed mother is expected – under the grants system – to contribute £103 a year to her training. 'She cannot afford this – I have to manage without' says Linda who has no money for any social life.

Headlines like 'Union Raps Low-grant "Scrooges",' 'Scandal of the Students Living on Chips', 'Grants Rule "Forcing Student Mothers into Vice"' were commonplace features of the *Daily Express* throughout 1973 and early 1974. Then, abruptly, the line changed again. Students were all right; but their leaders were hateful. The *Daily Express* on 4 December 1974, rigged together a story headed

ARE YOU SICK OF STUDENTS?
Bruce Kemble reports on one man fighting for the true
voice of our universities to be heard above the extremists.

It was a flimsy story about an obscure student politician
who disagreed with some decisions made at a recent N.U.S.
annual conference. The very next day there was another story
saying much the same thing:

STUDENT LEFT SENT DOWN
Now the moderates stand up to be counted.
As we said yesterday . . . Now even our students are becom-
ing sick of students. (By Garth Pearce)

The newspeg this time was that some student union posts at
Essex University were now filled by 'moderates'. One should
beware of attributing plots to the Press, but the suddenness
of the change of editorial policy coming so soon after the
appointment of a new editor – Alastair Burnett – can hardly
be dismissed as coincidence. John Randall the N.U.S.
President, in a speech to University students at Essex in
January 1975, described in detail what had happened.

. . . On 15th November last year we mounted our biggest
ever grants demonstration. That morning in the *Daily Express* there appeared a major feature article clearly designed
to imply that a grants increase was totally unnecessary, and
that the views of the N.U.S. were unrepresentative of the ordinary student. The article was based upon an interview
with a Bristol University student named 'Mark Roberts'.
Mr Roberts felt that he was well off, and implied that a
grants campaign was unnecessary. In general, his thinking
closely coincided with that of the *Daily Express*. Perhaps this
is hardly surprising. There is no record of a Mark Roberts
being registered at Bristol, nor does he appear on any of the
faculty lists. Did the *Express*, having failed to find a student
prepared to give voice to their prejudices, simply invent
one? I feel entitled to ask how many other comments made
in 'interviews' with the *Express* that echo so faithfully that
paper's editorial line emanate from non-existent persons.

In the week that followed the Margate conference last month, the *Express* mounted a major attack on the N.U.S. All the usual ingredients were there. The resolution passed on civil liberties was taken as evidence that we are all degenerate druggies. Our views on women's rights indicated extreme promiscuity and immorality. Secret Marxist cliques were uncovered. The drinking of toasts at the Russian Embassy (in Vodka of course) was hinted at. Even the red colour of the hair of a past president of the Union took on a political significance.

But in addition to this rather tired concoction of malicious tittle-tattle, the *Express* decided to cash in on the public emotion that had followed the Birmingham bombings. On the Tuesday following the [November 1974] conference the *Daily Express* had reported accurately the overwhelming rejection of support for the I.R.A. that had resulted from the conference debate on Ireland. Two days later the *Express* made a complete about face and claimed that 'Among the motions passed at the conference were support for the I.R.A.' For the second time, the *Express* had decided that facts should not be allowed to distort their opinions. If a downright lie was necessary to sustain the entirely false image of the N.U.S. that they were carefully constructing, then a downright lie would be printed. These are strong words, but they are backed by strong evidence. It could have been that the second *Express* story was a mistake. In this case one would have expected an immediate retraction when the error was drawn to the attention of the Editor. However, this has not been forthcoming, and all available evidence indicates that the misrepresentation is deliberate. There is reason to suspect that some of the emotive phraseology employed in certain of the articles was not contained in the original piece written by the paper's education correspondent, but was inserted at the insistence of more senior staff. As for the contradiction between the *Express*'s original accurate report and its subsequent distortions, correspondence with the Editor of the *Express* suggests that this was far from being a mistake.

What seems to have happened is that a new campaign had

been launched by a newspaper – a campaign to change the leadership of a national union. Now, there is no harm in that. Anyone is entitled to say that he believes that such-and-such a union leader is unfit to hold his post and his members ought to remove him. The Editor and proprietor of the *Daily Express*, by virtue of owning and controlling a national newspaper, can, of course, say it to a rather larger number of people than most of us. They therefore have considerable power within any democratic organisation. They can hammer their views home in huge type and short, emotive sentences. More important, they present the news: they state implicitly, so that it will be believed, that one man's view is important (although his members have not elected him to any important position) and another (who has been so elected) has views which are not important. They say what the news is and what it is not. This is a power the like of which no democratic politician has ever had. Over the past few years many trade unions have elected left-wing leaderships and taken left-wing decisions, and the A.U.E.W., the T.G.W.U., even the journalists' own union, the N.U.J., have suddenly found that the press is running a slanted, dishonest campaign to persuade the membership to change their leadership or their decision.

That is what happened among students, and that is the reason for the new approach of the *Daily Express* to student affairs. Its object is to achieve an N.U.S., and for that matter an A.U.E.W., a T.G.W.U., an N.U.J., and a T.U.C. which does, broadly speaking, what the press tells it to do.

The campaign was partly successful. Coincidentally (for all I can prove) the *Daily Express*'s groundwork in 1974 was followed by the first determined effort by the Conservative Party to take over the N.U.S. By 1976 the Federation of Conservative Students was able to boast a brace of student union presidents up and down the country and one member on the N.U.S. 17-strong National Executive.

The Conservative initiative was well-planned, well-publicised and, of course, well-financed. It was also well supported by the Press, which reported in detail their minutest advance. At the same time a few student unions decided to leave the N.U.S. because of its 'left-wing domination'. N.U.S. leaders – the strongest group was and is the Broad Left alliance of Labour and Communist Party members – became seriously alarmed, and their statements and attitudes reflected, in their growing moderation, the seriousness with which they took the supposed move to the right among students.

Political movements in unions are often gradual, because of the democratic processes which have to be gone through, and in the N.U.S. it has been so gradual that many people have still not noticed. Newspapers, labouring under no such democratic difficulties, change overnight. That is what happened this year, when the *Express* went tabloid and decided to look for younger readers. In February 1977 N.U.S. Secretary Sue Slipman was the subject of a thoroughly sympathetic write-up in the *Express* and it took all her persuasiveness even to get the paper to mention the fact that she is a member of the Communist Party.

The line has thus changed again: newspaper economics, fleetingly, have triumphed over a political campaign. But lest left-wing student leaders think their problems are over, perhaps I should quote from Lord Beaverbrook's evidence to the Royal Commission on the Press in 1948:

> My purpose originally was to set up a propaganda paper, and I have never deviated from that purpose all through the years.

A journalist now working for the *Daily Mirror*, with twenty-five years of Fleet Street reporting behind him, describes himself and his colleagues as 'willing whores'. It's not, he says, that news desks, news editors or editors say to their reporters: Go away and write a lie, go away and distort the truth. It's just that reporters know what is expected of them.

He tells a story of which he is still ashamed. In 1956 he was working for the *Daily Mail*, and was put on to General Election coverage. So one day he found himself in a large, drafty hall in Watford listening to Aneurin Bevan. It was a brilliant speech, he says. But at the end of the meeting, he knew what was expected of him. He sought out a woman in the audience who had shouted something at Bevan. His report the next morning in the *Daily Mail* began: 'A lone old age pensioner dared to challenge the might of Aneurin Bevan yesterday . . .' He was congratulated by his news editor.

The question to ask journalists is not: when did your news desk instruct you to give stories a misleading slant? It is: how often have you given stories a misleading slant because you are a good enough professional to know what your news desk wanted? It is journalists who have to provide the propaganda copy that, in the old days, the great crusading newspaper magnates provided themselves. The blunt instrument of propaganda used in the thirties by the Beaverbrook and Rothermere press has been replaced by a more effective, more insidious means of newspaper propaganda. The open use of the power of the newspapers is now discredited. 'You supply the photographs', the great American newspaper magnate William Randolph Hearst cabled to his correspondent in Havana in the 1890s 'and I'll supply the war' – and he did supply the war.

But simply because it is not done these days to boast openly of your power as a newspaper proprietor, there is no reason to suppose that newspapers have stopped supplying wars. In *The Newspaper Game* Paul Hoch outlines the way in which American newspapers have helped to supply the cold war, the Korean War and the Vietnam war. Today, newspapers still supply wars. They do not supply them by editorialising. They do not use the conventional methods of political parties, pressure groups and so on. They supply wars by slanting news evaluation and news presentation.

In theory, the professional skill of news editors and sub-editors is the skill of knowing what the readers will be interested in, what is important, how to present it interestingly. And that, frequently, is precisely what they do. It would be wrong to suppose that journalists are nothing more than cogs in a conspiracy. The major part of their professional life is spent in using their skill and experience to find out what is going on and write it up readably. But if a newspaper commits itself to a campaign, and if that newspaper is prepared to use any sort of distortion to make that campaign effective, in some way or another reporters, news editors and sub-editors,

- the house style'

however professional, however committed to honest journalism, are going to be drawn in.

Working journalists are in the front line. They make the
initial judgement about what news goes into newspapers.
Editors specifically committed to campaigns do not have to
tell them what the line is. They know. Tomorrow morning
buy the *Daily Mail, Daily Express, Daily Mirror* and *Sun* –
broadly speaking, the channel through which the British
working class find out what is going on in the world. The
chances are that at least three out of those four newspapers,
and quite possibly all four, have led off on the same news item.
It may be the most interesting and important thing that
happened yesterday, or it may not. That is a matter on which
you must use your judgement. But when you use that judgement, accept that it is a subjective one, for 'interest' and 'importance' are not objective concepts. The important thing is
that the editors of those newspapers have made the same
judgement.

Take a simple example – the day Princess Anne was
married. You do not need to be told what news every
newspaper decided its readers cared about most the following
day. The *Morning Star*, though, chose to make an interesting
point about the nature of newspapers. It led with some industrial news and, very low down on its front page, gave less
than a column inch to a tiny news item under the heading
'TRAFFIC DISRUPTED', which told *Morning Star* readers that
traffic had been blocked for several hours in central London
because of a royal wedding. Extend that principle.
Newspapers decide by the process of news selection what is
important. By their news selection over a long period, they
also decide what people, political parties, institutions are important, and they decide what those people, political parties
and organisations are like. When we say 'newspapers decide'
we do not mean that those who produce newspapers decide.
We mean that newspaper editors and proprietors decide.
Journalists use their professional techniques to implement
those decisions. Judgements, therefore, are made by
newspaper editors and proprietors. Too often the job of the
journalist is to implement those judgements in the presentation of the news he collects. Part of the apparatus given to him

with which to implement these judgements is a vocabulary full of stipulative definitions. What does 'moderate' mean? Or 'democratic'? Or 'militant', or 'rabble-rousing', or even 'drunk'? Humpty Dumpty had the best answer:

> 'When I use a word', said Humpty Dumpty, 'it means exactly what I want it to mean. Neither more nor less.'
> (Lewis Carroll, *Alice Through the Looking Glass*)

The role of the journalist is too frequently that of the man who painstakingly collects the news – the news his newspaper wants to hear; who, with professional skill, writes it up readably in the way his newspaper wants it written; whose trade is words – words whose definition is stipulated by his newspaper. That is not to say that journalists are mere ciphers. There are, and have always been, a great many journalists who have worked to present what they think is important in a way they believe to be fair and honest. On some newspapers – nationally, notably the *Guardian* – they are frequently allowed to get away with it. But it does mean that the journalist is an employee, whose living, like the living of a man on an assembly line, depends on pressing the right social and political levers. The techniques of the journalist can be weapons to be used to expose wrongdoing and injustice. They can also be the property of an unscrupulous employer who is in the fortunate position of possessing a near monopoly on information and the means of employing the best disseminators of that information.

I want now to try to answer three questions:

1. Do newspapers have power?
2. If they do, who controls that power?
3. Have those controllers earned the right to that power? Do they use it responsibly?

1. *Do newspapers have power?*

Few people now believe that the expressed views of a

newspaper are decisive in affecting the views of its readers. A newspaper's editorial column can thunder, yet even at general election time it probably hardly affects the result. But newspapers have a much greater, more insidious power than that. Newspapers decide what is news and how it is to be treated. Of all the things which happened yesterday, the newspapers will select which of those things merit a couple of paragraphs at the bottom of an inside page, and which of them don't matter at all, which to take seriously and which to send up. Sometimes newspapers give a great deal of coverage to an event which has no importance nor is especially interesting. You can say: there is nothing there, nothing has happened. You cannot say: there is no news, for news is what appears in newspapers, and therefore if the newspapers print the news, it is a mere tautology that the news exists. We can say that precious little happened. We cannot say that there was no news, for the news appeared in the newspapers. Newspapers do not tell us what to think about issues. They do something much more important and much more insidious: they tell us what the issues are. Newspapers define the parameters of respectable debate. And that is a terrible power. The man is truly playing God who has the power to say, not just 'X is good', but 'X is' or 'X is not'.

2. *Who controls that power?*

All journalistic staff are ultimately responsible to the editor, and he is responsible to the proprietor, who appoints him and can dismiss him. Alastair Burnett, until recently editor of the *Daily Express*, said on television this year that before the *Express* proprietor appointed him 'we had a very long chat and found ourselves broadly in agreement'. He left no doubt that if they had not found themselves 'broadly in agreement' he would not have been appointed. On the same television programme (*Inside the Press*) Mr Burnett delicately pointed to another pressure on the editor: 'advertisers have their standards', he said.

In 1956 the *Guardian*, alone among national newspapers, opposed the British invasion of Suez. Overnight, 40 per cent of the *Guardian*'s advertising revenue disappeared. Big business didn't like the *Guardian*'s view and was using its heavy weaponry to underline the point. *Guardian* editor Alastair Hetherington was allowed to continue with his policy, and over the next few years his *faux pas* was gradually forgotten and forgiven and the advertising came back in dribs and drabs. That is because the structure of ownership of the *Guardian* is different from that of any other Fleet Street newspaper. It is owned by a non-profit making trust and the editor can therefore occasionally afford to take a stand which advertisers dislike. No other Fleet Street editor could have got away with it. He would either have reversed his policy or been sacked.

These, then, are the two major pressures on editors: the pressure to please his proprietor, and the pressure not to offend big business from which his newspaper's lifeblood, its advertising revenue, comes. There are no other pressures so strong as these two. The pressures about which editors and proprietors complain most frequently – the pressures from print and journalistic trade unions – are comparatively insignificant. It is true that print unions have occasionally managed to prevent the appearance of material designed to be grossly offensive to their members in the newspapers which their labour produces: and it is true that this has occasionally resulted in complaints that they are hampering the freedom of the Press. These complaints assume that the Press was free to start with. So proprietors and advertisers have powers over editors. Those whose labour produces newspapers – journalists and printers – are almost entirely excluded from a share in that power. The other excluded category is consumers of newspapers. We hear frequently that if newspapers were totally out of step with the views of the people they cater for, those people would stop buying them. But newspapers, in so far as they are in touch with public opinion at all, are in touch with it by helping to mould it.

3. *Have they earned that power? Do they use it responsibly?*

You have certain experts in television, people who know about lighting, sound, interviewing. The interviewers then use that expertise to take political decisions – that industrial disputes will be discussed *ad nauseam* and not industrial safety, for example. It is the tyranny of selection and presentation. (Anthony Wedgwood Benn talking to the N.U.J.'s Press and Public Relations Branch, 1975)

The power of the Press is concentrated in the hands of a few, very rich men. Their interest is the maintenance of the *status quo*. They have proved many times that they are prepared to use their power ruthlessly to maintain what they see as their interests.

The pressure to make money brings with it the pressure to present packaged, pre-digested and therefore misleading news and the pressure not to offend advertisers and distributors.

The structure of the ownership of newspapers ensure that most mass-circulation newspapers will pursue editorial policies which are in the interests of the very rich, for it is the very rich who own them.

4

Trouble at t'Millpond – Farmworkers in the Media

Deputy Editor of Landworker – *journal of the National Union of Agricultural and Allied Workers*

The Ripon district of the National Union of Agricultural and Allied Workers was worried about filling the empty spaces in the darts team. 'What about the lads that work with you?' the man in the corner asked. He shook his head: 'They'll have nowt to do with union. They say it's no good.' A little later the conversation turned to the pay increase for Woolworth's salesgirls which gave them 50p more than farm labourers. 'You should work in Woolworth's,' someone cracked to the woman present. 'We should all work there,' someone else said.

The Times

The quote, believe it or not, is the introduction to a story about an industrial dispute: one of many thousands that must have appeared in the 'top people's paper' during 1975. Why it appears different, and what is unexpected about this particular story, is its element of humour.

For the most part newspapers display a morbid obsession with industrial disputes. The language is one of confrontation, creating the impression that the world of the industrial correspondent is a world of drama – full of 'strike threats', 'challenges', 'disruption'. But every now and then we glimpse another world – more of a tragi-comedy than a drama. This is the world of the low-paid worker: the dustman, the hospital porter and above all – as the quote from *The Times* well illustrates – the world of the farm labourer.

Poking fun at farm labourers is as old as journalism itself. In the early nineteenth century the contemptuous use of words like 'Hodge' to describe the farm labourer was already commonplace in the Press. Not until the formation of agricultural workers' unions in the last quarter of the nineteenth century did this attitude begin to change.

'They'll have nowt to do with union. They say it's no good.' The humour derives – after the fashion of a Shakespeare play – from these 'low characters' consistently failing in their aspirations. *The Times* goes on:

> Then, after an hour's discussion of the latest round of pay talks and the prospect of militancy, this small group of hard-working people with weather-beaten faces, who have never manned a picket line in their lives, quietly agreed to ask their union executive to prepare for industrial action.

The punchline is that

> With the exception of the Tolpuddle Martyrs, farm workers have not been famous for their militancy. The last strike was in Norfolk in 1923, when they prevented their wages being cut, since then they have shown their dissatisfaction with pay and conditions by leaving the land for jobs in the towns.

The farmworkers' grievances may be more important than the spaces in the darts team but, of course, to spell this out would ruin the joke. Instead, *The Times* has its own explanation for the upsurge in militant action:

> The focus for militants in the union is an elegant Georgian cottage in Thirsk, Yorkshire, with chintz curtains and a large portrait of Lenin over the mantelpiece. From there Miss Joan Maynard, county chairman and Labour M.P. for Sheffield Brightside, talks of food strikes involving workers from farm to shop, and action on the country's 59 company farms, which each employ 100 men or more.

The alarming prospect of food strikes led by somebody with a portrait of Lenin over the mantelpiece is soon dispelled, however. Reassuringly *The Times* says: 'Compared to other industries, agriculture is badly organised . . . On small farms the owner usually works alongside his one or two men, creating an intimate relationship into which it is difficult for a union to penetrate.' And then there are tied cottages: 'A man will think twice before crossing his employer if he fears not only will he lose his job, but his home as well.'

The cynicism of these remarks reflects a view of the farmworkers' struggle best summed up by Rex C. Russell, when he wrote of the early farmworkers' unions: 'Nobody in the middle and upper classes believed that farmworkers had the initiative, the courage, or the ability to think, act, and organise for himself' (Rex C. Russell, 'The Revolt of the Field in Lincolnshire', Lincs. County Committee N.U.A.W., 1947). In a similar vein, on 16 September 1975, under a headline 'Farmworkers' wives are in a militant mood', *The Times* said: 'If the Agricultural Wages Board fails to respond generously to the wage claim to be presented today by the National Union of Agricultural Workers it might have a long struggle on its hands. For the first time, the wives of farmworkers are showing signs of militancy and determination to back their husbands to the hilt over pay.' Quoting one of the wives, the report continued: 'Her husband and his younger workmates are already beginning to talk about striking.' But ' "The union does not seem to have much go", she said. "The trouble is that members are too spread out for them striking".'

Earlier, on 19 June, the *Sun* went out of its way to convey the same message. Under a headline 'Unrest is growing down on the farm': first, the shock, horror, introduction, 'The National Union of Agricultural and Allied Workers has the power to hold the country to ransom by starvation.' Then, ignoring the 1910 Norfolk strike, a strike in Lancashire in 1914, strikes in Essex and elsewhere in 1914, a 1920 strike in Yorkshire, and a strike in Norfolk in 1923 – when the union issued 10,000 strike notices – the *Sun* goes on: 'But the Union, formed in 1906, has never called a national farmworkers' strike.' It says, though: 'If there was a walkout, the shops would soon run out of food, and milk supplies would dry up.' But 'This unique industrial power has never been exercised because many workers have a loyalty to their farmer bosses. And they also care deeply about the animals they look after. The problems of organising industrial action would also be immense, because farmworkers are scattered so widely throughout Britain.'

The contradictions – they are 'scattered so widely' throughout the story – have the effect of obscuring the issue, and increase the difficulty of making sense of the farmworkers' action. The immense problem for the *Sun* reader, then, is one of understanding. And yet the suggestion that the farmworkers' union is trying, albeit unsuccessfully, to stir up rural discontent is somehow curiously explicit. But the *Sun* is not unique in that. There is never any suggestion, though, that strike action might be a legitimate way to settle workers' grievances.

The sentiments are expressed rather differently nowadays, but the general attitude seems to have changed little since 'The Radical Programme' (reprinted in Rex. C. Russell, 1947) issued nearly ninety years ago by a group of Liberal Party members, declared of the farm labourer:

> It is true that he is often treated with condescending kindness, and as a deserving object of charity and benevolence, so long – and only so long – as he is docile and subservient, but any attempt at self-assertion or independence is punished and put down by the many forms of social persecution which are in the hands of his superiors. Propertyless and with no security of house and home, he has no means of helping himself and any attempt of others to help him – except by social or benevolent means – is felt to be, and is frequently described as, a criminal attempt to unsettle the minds of happy and contented men and to set class against class.

Contemporary newspapers would certainly avoid using the word 'class' apart from telling readers 'we are all middle class now' – a patently absurd proposition when applied to farmworkers. Where today they might allude to 'a portrait of Lenin over the mantelpiece', newspaper reports in the nineteenth century, though just as ludicrous, were more direct. In 1872, one of the founders of the National

Agricultural Workers' Union, Joseph Arch, was accused of being a 'Jesuit in disguise'. The union whose leaders described its aims as neither 'republican nor communistic' but merely for 'just wages, proper house and accommodation', was denounced by the Bishop of Gloucester at the Gloucester Agricultural Society's dinner on 2 August 1872. A full report appeared in *The Times* of 6 August, quoting the Bishop's belief that 'mischievous and evil efforts were being made to set class against class, and especially to set faithful agricultural labourers against their faithful English employers'.

Much of the present day coverage is entirely consistent with this view of farmworkers as 'happy and contented men' and 'faithful agricultural labourers'. A report in the *Daily Express* in February 1975 headlined 'The £30 pay gap in the pay-day league' went on to disclose 'My life by man at bottom', and stated:

> Farmworker Fred Durham, aged 40, is married with five children. The family live in a tied farm cottage in Kent. Mr Durham earns about £30 basic and by putting in six or eight hours of overtime at this time of year, takes home about £36 a week. He hands it all over to his wife Evelyn. She spends up to £25 on food, £4 to a savings club for clothes, and the rest on electricity, gas and coal. Mr Durham said 'I don't think much about people who get paid more than I do. It doesn't affect me. I work at a farm where I get paid a bit over the minimum rate. I think we're well off.'

However, a rather different picture does emerge from time to time. In 1974 the National Union of Agricultural and Allied Workers submitted a claim for a £35 basic wage for farmworkers, at a time when farmworkers' earnings were at least £12 a week less than other manual workers, and £17 a week less than the average for all employed workers. But after a prolonged negotiating session on 12 December, no settlement was reached on an offer of £27.80 – £1.60 on the then basic of £26.20 – and the union negotiators walked out of the meeting. Another meeting was hurriedly fixed for 23 December. It may have been the season of goodwill, but at this meeting the previous offer was only marginally increased, and a pay award of £28.50 from January, with a further £2 increase from July, was carried through on the votes of the 'independent members' of the national negotiating body.

Union members were apprehensive about the possible outcome of the negotiations: it had been predicted that inflation would increase by more than 25 per cent during the following year, the period covered by the settlement, and anger had been mounting throughout November and early December. Immediately after the session on 12 December, the union negotiators returned to the head office in Gray's Inn Road for an emergency meeting of the Executive Committee, called to discuss the offer and the prospect of industrial action.

Next day the papers were full of headlines like 'Farmworkers threaten to halt milk supplies' (*Daily Express*) and 'Strike on the farm looms over pay talks'. 'Farmworkers are prepared to disrupt milk supplies to enforce their claim for a basic £30 per week', screamed the *Express* on 28 December. The *Express* had got the amount wrong – £30 instead of £35 – which made it seem that the farmworkers' action was over a mere £2.20, less than a third of the £7.20 that the argument was really about. But it went on: 'Miss Joan Maynard, Labour M.P. for Sheffield Brightside, and a Yorkshire Secretary of the Union, said yesterday, "Industrial action is long overdue".' On 25 January, under the headline 'Farm strike threat to shopping bag', the *Express* warned readers,

Milk and fresh food supplies could be threatened by strike action by Britain's 260,000 farmworkers. They are angry that the farm wages board rejected demands for a £35 minimum wage. Leaders of the Agricultural Workers' Union will meet in London next week to consider what action to take. Some of the 300 local branches want a series of mass demonstrations, one day strikes, or disruption of supplies of milk, fruit and vegetables. More seriously, some want a national stoppage in the spring. This would prevent the sowing of vital potato and cereal crops.

The story ended on an even more sinister note: 'Other areas

have called for selective strikes which would be kept secret until the last moment.'

Earlier on 29 December, the *Sunday Telegraph* had warned: 'Militant farmworkers are planning to blockade fruit and vegetable markets and dairies to prevent produce reaching the public as a protest against low wages.' On the use of scab labour, it declared even more threateningly: 'Moves by some farmers to hire non-union drivers should the farmworkers' plans go ahead "will only lead to increased trouble", a union spokesman said.' The *Daily Telegraph* took up the theme on 30 December: under a headline 'Blockade on food urged' it said: 'Farmworkers are being urged by militants to blockade fruit and vegetable markets and dairies to stop milk and fresh food reaching the shops.' And it quoted Tom Torney, Labour M.P. for Bradford South and Chairman of the Food and Agriculture Committee of M.P.s as saying, 'I am seriously concerned that the nation's food supplies, particularly milk, could be threatened. The farmworkers are in angry mood and mean business this time.'

Where in all this were the workers who 'have a loyalty to their farmer bosses' and 'care deeply about the animals'? The *Daily Telegraph* was as predictable as ever with its mention of 'militants' urging farmworkers to 'stop milk and fresh food reaching the shops'. And throughout this dispute, farmworkers found themselves getting the kind of treatment usually reserved for more unruly elements – the car workers, the dockers and the miners. Farmworkers wanted a national stoppage in the spring, mass demonstrations, blockades of fruit and vegetable markets, or they threatened the poor old shopping bag. They were 'angry at the farm wages board'. But the newspapers did not exactly go out of their way to spell out the employers' share of responsibility; that had it not been for the employers' intransigence at the wages board negotiations the nation's food supplies might not have been threatened.

In fact, rather the opposite was the case, as the *Express* indicated in its piece on 28 December:

Meanwhile their employers are threatening to take to the street again in 1975 unless the government acts to save the industry from bankruptcy. Mr Myrrdin Evans, President of the Farmers' Union of Wales, says in a New Year message to members: 'My fear is they will not be so easily persuaded to confine their activities to orderly demonstrations.'

It is all right for the employers to take to the streets, apparently, but if the workers do likewise it is altogether a different matter. And what must the *Daily Telegraph*'s readers have made of the suggestion of increased trouble were the employers to try breaking the strike by hiring non-union labour? That the farmworkers were about to bring society as we know it to an end?

The dispute had arisen out of the workers' specific grievance over the pay increase doled out by the Agricultural Wages Board, but the real implications of the Wages Board's action were almost wholly ignored. It was left to Frank Field, director of the Child Poverty Action Group, to spell out some of the details in an article in the *New Statesman*, a paper not generally regarded as having a large working-class readership. He pointed out the pay award would mean a drastic cut in farmworkers' living standards: 'This is the prospect after a year during which farmworkers with children saw a significant decline in their already inadequate living standards.'

And yet, two months later, the *Daily Express* was telling readers all about Fred Durham, aged forty, with his family of five children, who thought he was well off. Where was Fred Durham on 10 November 1975, when the farmworkers again made the headlines with 'Families who live in poverty on the farm' (*Daily Mail*), 'Hunger on the Farms Scandal' (*Daily Mirror*), 'Rural poverty crisis' (*Daily Telegraph*) and 'Families who can't afford to eat breakfast' (the *Express*). A report by the Low Pay Unit, an offshoot of the Child Poverty Action Group, had shown 'Thousands of farmworkers cannot afford to feed themselves or their families properly', the *Express* disclosed.

The report claims that average earnings on farms are 30 per cent below the level in factories, and the margin is not made up by fringe benefits such as low rents and cheap food . . . Nearly half the farmworkers and their wives interviewed went without breakfast, says the report. And two thirds of the children over five years old had no pocket money and more than half the families could not afford holidays.

The *Mail* stated: 'Comments from workers and wives present a grim picture of some families living in cold, cheerless, slum conditions, paying substantially more for food and other necessities and existing on inadequate diets.'

It hardly seemed credible that such conditions could exist. And certainly, what the papers described as the Low Pay Unit's 'claims' were quickly shattered: 'Mr John Davies, chairman of the Employment Committee of the National Farmers' Union, said yesterday that the report was a total distortion' (*Daily Express*). 'Mr John Davies, chairman of the National Farmers' Union employment committee said: "The statements in the report are so far from the truth they destroy any credibility in the Unit" ' (*Daily Mail*). *The Times*, always a day late, headlined a separate story on 11 November: 'Farmers query validity of pay report.' And the *Financial Times*, also on 11 November, disclosing 'Farmers upset by call for £6', said: 'Farmers' leaders hit out yesterday at the findings of a survey, published by the Low Pay Unit, which called for the £6 increase allowable under the Government's wages policy to be granted to agricultural workers.'

As it was, the farmworkers got their £6 at a meeting of the Agricultural Wages Board on 17 November. Although the agreement was not to be implemented until 20 January 1976, and the value was somewhat reduced when tied cottage rents were increased by up to £1, the jump from £30.50 to £36.50 was the biggest increase the farmworkers had ever had. But everybody else was getting a £6 rise, so the settlement did nothing to narrow the gap between farmworkers' earnings and those in industry. It wouldn't have done to make this too obvious, perhaps. The *Sun* went one better on 24 November: 'Even after their new £6 rise, farmworkers will still be among the lowest paid in the country. Does life on the farm mean too many sacrifices? Or is it worth it to escape the city smoke?' Never mind the families 'living in cold, cheerless, slum conditions . . . existing on inadequate diets'. That is not something the newspapers like wholly to admit, especially when the farmworkers engage in militant action to change their conditions. Such action is not seen or presented as a reasonable response to low pay and poverty. This is so even when the Press have acknowledged elsewhere how bad those conditions are. The attitude has not therefore changed: farmworkers are to be pitied and perhaps should be the subject of benevolent attention, but the Lord protect us if they assert their rights in a manner which might set class against class!

On the whole, it seems that farmworkers are treated largely as a joke. But the humour is misplaced and contradictory. Just as their putting up with poor wages and bad conditions is made to seem tragi-comic, so they are both pitied and derided at the same time. They are patronised for being loyal and hardworking, but this image conflicts with the other image as militants holding the country to ransom. Newspapers attempt to get round these contradictions by denying the legitimacy of the farmworkers' grievances, by quoting the denials of the farm employers as fact, or by using other devices, like mentioning the wives' attitude rather than letting the men speak for themselves. The alternative would be to recognise that the farmworkers' militancy was the result of their poor wages and bad conditions. To do that, of course, would mean taking them seriously. And that is what newspapers generally refuse to do.

5

The Production of Trade Union News

TONI GRIFFITHS

Press Officer at the National and Local Government Officers' Association

Trade unionists often say that you should never believe what you read in the newspapers. This cynicism comes from a feeling that what is read in the newspapers or seen on the television is often not 'like real life'. Even so, some trade unionists can still react sharply to the suggestion that news may not be neutral, even when presented with evidence that television news can distort reality. Often such evidence is felt to be threatening and is taken as an accusation of previous gullibility.

It is not surprising then to find that the news organisations themselves are highly defensive when issues of objectivity or bias are raised. For them, it is as though any implication that news may be anything less than neutral constitutes a personal attack on the integrity and professionalism of the journalists involved.

What makes trade unionists particularly sensitive to the picture of the industrial world they get from newspapers, television and radio is precisely that it *is* a picture, one picture among several possible pictures. And it is a picture presented as reality. Trade unionists probably feel this more than most since they tend to suffer more than most from the way in which the news picture of the world is derived. It may be that the nature of these attitudes to news is a response to the frustrating elusiveness of the process whereby an event is transformed into news. This involves the permeation of the event by a specific attitude towards the world and it becomes news when it can be assigned a significance in accordance with what is defined as being important. Newspapers frequently claim that they present their news in accordance with ideas (commercially derived) of what the reader wants. This often means that information is distilled through a series of stereotypes and the result is often over-simplification and distortion. The result is a strengthening of prejudices about how society is ordered and how groupings within society work – for example, how economic crises are 'caused' and the role of the trade unions in these crises. The point is brought home in this tongue-in-cheek news story from the *Morning Star* (12 November 1975): 'Wildcat Tory peers carried their wrecking tactics to new extremes last night.'

These media viewpoints are composed of certain notions of established truth which are rarely stated explicitly but which, nevertheless, underpin news reporting. They are the agents that determine how events are transformed into news. Thus a strike is almost always to be deplored and is against good sense; and it is news, where years of negotiation are not. Similarly, the background and reasons for a strike are unlikely to get much coverage. For example, 200 NALGO members employed by the British Waterways Board took strike action in 1974 following an unsatisfactory final pay offer. The background involved an erosion of real incomes, the effects of reorganisation, relativities with other groups, traditions of non-militancy and inadequate working conditions. Of the 800 column inches of press coverage studied, 715 were devoted to the progress of the strike and 15 were devoted to the background (or why the strike was necessary in the first place).

Discussing 'why trade unions do not get fair hearing' Bryan Magee, Labour M.P. for Waltham Forest Leyton, wrote:

Most journalists and broadcasters see society from a middle class point of view, and all the travesties I have instanced are aspects of the same uncomprehending, not to say frightened, caricature of industrial trade unionism which is now common currency in middle class thought. Another cause is that trade union affairs are thought to be boring, with the consequence that they are written up in terms of personalities and confrontations instead of issues, committee elections and the things that actually matter. (*The Times*, 10 November 1975)

Most trade unionists do not 'like' going on strike, nor do they 'like' being on the dole, but the prominence given these activities through news values presents them almost as though they did. Events appear unreasonable unless placed in their own true context. Trade union elections are a case in point. The over-simplified coverage given to the activities and beliefs of individuals standing for election must influence union elections. An interesting sidelight on how people see and relate to such elections was given towards the end of 1976 when the NALGO press officer was telephoned by a firm of City stockbrokers wanting to know about future union elections – so that 'records could be updated'. During conversation, it emerged that the real interest lay in the election of a successor to Jack Jones at the Transport and General Workers' Union and the ensuing ripple that it was assumed would affect the state of the £. The City seemed to be preparing for an attack of the vapours well in advance. Newspaper headline writers suffer regularly from the same phenomenon. These headlines, for example, presented a distorted picture of NALGO – 'Reds under the Bed row rocks NALGO' (*Sunday Sun*), 'Fight to save NALGO from Red Wreckers' (*Daily Mail*) – when the basis of the story was one individual's view of the activities of a group of radical NALGO members. Journalists often dissociate themselves from the headlines over their stories; nevertheless, it is the total presentation of an event or policy that sticks in the reader's mind and reinforces a particular view of the world. This is particularly important in defining the framework of economic stories: 'Dole queue threat will bring unions into line' (*Daily Telegraph*); 'As the town hall big spenders are called to heel' (*Evening Standard*); 'Public sector has "crowded out" private borrowing' (*Financial Times*). Each of these headlines incorporates assumptions about the working of the economy which have been selected for prominent display. They inevitably establish a framework for perceiving the news.

The coverage of different trade unions is related more to news values than to their actual contributions. NALGO is a large union – the fourth largest (683,000) in the T.U.C. and the biggest white-collar union in the world. Although it puts a lot into press work, it is not perceived as a main source of news. Its traditions are non-militant (although there is an increasing number of examples of industrial action) and it is one of the 'second generation' of T.U.C. unions. These may be among the reasons why its news prestige may be seen as lower than that of say the N.U.M. One journalist denied that the unions were viewed differently as potential news sources until he remembered that his own newspaper invariably sent the less senior industrial correspondent to cover NALGO conferences. Only a handful of general secretaries are consistently asked to comment on significant developments in the economy. With developments like the Social Contract in recent years, the role of those trade union leaders who negotiate with the government – the 'Neddy Six' (that is the T.U.C. representatives on the National Economic Development Council) – is larger than ever. Trade union thinking and reaction can be located by the media much more easily in this group and it has become the reference point in stories about the economy and the role of the unions in any developments. Thus, the wide range of views, feelings and policies within a body of eleven million people is often located by the media in the 'Neddy Six'.

There is a consensus amongst the media, about what is important (for example public spending – there should be less), whose views matter (the Treasury's) what the unions will take (ask the 'Neddy Six'). This consensus diminishes the role of other important interests, for example different views about public spending from the Cambridge school of economists and strong views within the T.U.C. about the need for more, not less, public spending in order to strengthen industry. This is inhibiting because unions whose views or policies may be different to, or more strident than, those views presented as the T.U.C.'s tend to refrain from appearing to 'rock the boat'. Unions which do pursue policies more stridently than at the consensus pace are seen as either 'maverick' or 'unrealistic'. And the label is influential. For example, the public sector unions did not ask for official T.U.C. support for a big demonstration and lobby of Parliament on cuts in public spending and unemployment in November 1976. It was thought better not to ask than to risk a public refusal. So the 'mavericks' often have to go to extreme lengths to gain a hearing or to have their views quoted. They are not treated all that seriously. The *Daily Telegraph's* news coverage of the November demonstrations began, 'Although 40,000 people took the day off yesterday to demonstrate against government cuts, few council or hospital services seemed to be affected.' The framework was immediately established. Obviously, the demonstration attracted a lot of coverage, but the *Sun* provided less than 100 words and the *Daily Mirror* devoted 135 words on page 15. The *Daily Express* gave 150 words to the demonstration, with a lengthy leader denigrating public service workers.

An interesting aspect of the coverage was the estimate of the numbers taking part in the national demonstration. Newspaper reports gave various estimates, ranging from 20,000 to 80,000. Trade union organisers' estimates varied between 60,000 and 80,000. One NALGO member queried the B.B.C. coverage on the day. The 7 p.m. radio news bulletin said that the demonstration had involved 15,000 to 20,000 and the newsreader emphasised that this was half the turnout anticipated by the organisers. The NALGO member telephoned the B.B.C. and was told that these were the Metropolitan Police figures. She pointed out that the *Evening Standard* four hours earlier had cited police estimates of more than 40,000. On the B.B.C. 1 *Nine o'clock News*, the figure was 20,000. The NALGO member telephoned the press bureau at New Scotland Yard, asked what figure had been given to the B.B.C. and was told 40,000 plus. The B.B.C. news desk was telephoned, but was engaged. On telephoning the following morning, the duty officer explained that the B.B.C. also had their reporters on the demonstration. The NALGO member pointed out that on the late news at 11.30 p.m. the proper police figures were broadcast, but that most people were probably in bed by that time.

The mutually reinforcing relationship between the media and the social system is well illustrated in the coverage of the economic crises of 1976. The coverage was characterised by a skilful series of Treasury briefings of the media which prepared the way – in a calculated manner – for the public spending announcements in February, April, July, November and December. By the time the cuts came, everyone was so 'prepared' for their inevitability that any serious alternative or opposition was disarmed. Even a vote against the government in the House of Commons could be shrugged off (which may encourage cynicism about what it is possible to achieve through discussion and argument).

Unions like NALGO, and the T.U.C. (in its Congress policy and Economic Review) had developed a case against economic policies of cuts and recession. They argued for selective, short-term import controls, the channelling of money to productive investment, control of money flows in this country and abroad and high levels of public spending to stimulate demand and provide jobs. The case was argued in detailed economic reviews from individual unions and was made independently by outside economists, but little sustained attention was given to the alternative economic strategy. Often it was stigmatised as a 'siege economy' and, in the case of the public sector unions, the economic case was frequently dismissed as a front for saving the jobs of bureaucrats. Items in news bulletins do not encourage alternative explanations of the cause and solution of economic problems: the Treasury thinking inevitably permeated the news. For example, one of the main public planks of the Treasury's economic plans was to cut public spending in order to 'transfer resources' from the public sector to manufacturing. This is what viewers of the B.B.C. 2 programme *Newsday* were told at 7.30 p.m. on 26 November 1976:

And with negotiations with the I.M.F. now at a critical stage, a Treasury Minister, Mr Joel Barnett, has warned that large numbers of people will have to leave their jobs in central and local government to work in industry. In the last ten years, civil servants and local government workers have increased by more than $\frac{1}{4}$ million whilst industry has lost 1 million workers. Mr Barnett says public spending has grown faster than the rate of economic growth can sustain, and this has been a major reason for Britain's economic decline.

An easily understandable image: instead of getting off the train from Sevenoaks to Charing Cross, all those chaps in bowler hats will have to clock in at the mill and start producing exports.

Joel Barnett's office was contacted but his staff said that the B.B.C. had 'misrepresented' the Minister's speech. They had no idea where there were the manufacturing jobs to which people were to go. (This was not surprising: a senior Treasury official, Alan Lord, had said at York on 10 November, 'In the short run, this means that for a given output we shall need a good deal less labour and new investment so that there will be an increase in the underlying rate of unemployment.')

The B.B.C. was later contacted. The Treasury, it transpired, had not complained about the 'misrepresentation'. Then the B.B.C. wrote as follows: 'I fear we did not adequately convey the sense of Joel Barnett's speech in our 7.30 p.m. *Newsday* bulletin. Our own specialists [not, to the best of my knowledge, the Treasury directly] had spotted this and advised the Assistant Editor accordingly.'

As a result, a more adequate (and precise!) version appeared in the *Nine o'clock News* on B.B.C. 1, and in the *Late News* on B.B.C. 2 on Friday 26 November 1976. This was the later version on the *Nine o'clock News*:

The departure of the I.M.F. team has been put back a week because Ministers haven't *yet* found it easy to swallow the medicine our international bank managers would like the Chancellor to prescribe. Mr Barnett – whose job it is to watch public spending – today gave us a taste of what's in store. First, getting people out of the civil service and local government – and into industry – a situation whereby – as the Chief Secretary put it – in the last 10 years the number of employees in manufacturing industry has fallen from 8.4 million to 7.33 million while in national and local government service – not including teachers or health service workers – the number has risen from 1.3 to 1.6 million.

This Treasury theme of 'transferring resources' by big cuts recurred consistently, despite the fact that the Treasury's own information showed that it was economically unviable and despite mounting unemployment.

On 3 December there was an inspired story in the *Guardian* suggesting that the Treasury was about to win again in its battle for cuts (and therefore more unemployment). Readers were now being adjusted to accept cuts of £1.500 million. In the event, cuts of £1,000 million in 1977/78 were announced on 15 December. The unions, particularly NALGO, had been pointing out that cuts meant fewer jobs, less growth, more inflation, less investment, but the cuts were continually and successfully presented by the Treasury as the 'only way out' for Britain. *Plus ça change: plus la meme chose*: On 22 February 1925 Winston Churchill had commented in a memorandum:

> The Treasury has never, it seems to me, faced the profound significance of what Mr Keynes calls 'the paradox of unemployment amidst dearth'. The governor shows himself perfectly happy in the spectacle of Britain possessing the finest credit in the world simultaneously with a million and a quarter unemployed . . . The community lacks goods, and a million and a quarter people lack work . . . The Treasury and the Bank of England policy has been the only policy consistently pursued. It is a terrible responsibility for those who have shaped it . . .

The Treasury set the economic framework of the coverage and the unions had difficulty in getting across an alternative economic case. For example, London Weekend Television broadcast a detailed account of Britain's economic problems and ideas for their solution in its *Weekend World* programme on 12 December 1976. An interview with NALGO's research officer, which outlined the merits of alternative economic policies, was scrapped from this programme. *Weekend World* wrote apologising for the omission which had occurred because of 'pressures of time'. The traditionalists, steered through the programme by Peter Jay, Economics Editor of *The Times*, had a clear field, unhindered by pressures of time.

It should be stressed that the argument is not that a particular alternative way of looking at things should permeate the news, but that alternative views which are known to exist, to be held by significant numbers of people and to be available in an articulate form should, as a matter of right, be given broadcast time. During the economic events of 1976, the alternative economic strategy proposed by the unions was hardly given a fair hearing. The news and its presentation were heavily coloured by the Treasury view of the economy and its publicly expressed solution to the economic crisis (cuts in public spending and wage restraint). Looking at the coverage as a whole, adherents of the alternative solutions were not treated seriously. This is in spite of many initiatives taken by NALGO, for example, to argue its economic case in public. Letters were published and several accounts appeared, but they stood little chance of forming part of the framework of reference for news stories on the economy in the way that Treasury orthodoxy did.

NALGO had mounted a campaign against cuts in public spending and its economic case was mentioned when it could be linked to a demonstration or lobby or a news 'event'. But such coverage is 'flash in the pan': it fades in the glare of the news framework set up in the orthodox or establishment light. This framework made wage restraint and public spending levels two of the essential and unchanging criteria by which the significance of economic discussion and initiative was measured, although there were other criteria which could have formed part of the continuous framework of reference – for example, the chronic failure of British industry to seize the opportunities provided for investment, or the speculative and erratic flow of money within this country and abroad. Journalism, of course, is said to be concerned with 'hard facts' and it has been observed that an important determinant of 'fact' is the proven reliability of the source. Yet it has been shown that, in industrial stories, the source of the 'facts' is often the government or the management – on or off the record – and the union side is looked to for 'events', usually demonstrations, strikes, pickets.

Another aspect of this phenomenon is given in a study of the Press in local politics, *The Silent Watchdog: the Press in Local Politics* by D. Murphy (Constable, 1976). Pressure groups for example, welcome Press coverage, but local newspapers tend to report them only after they have appeared in council

minutes – the main source of local political news. So they obtain validation as a source of news *through* the council, not over
its head. They thus enter the area of news–reportable society.

It is often said that the trade unions are covered when they
do 'newsworthy' things, but in terms of what is defined as
news this leaves out a good deal of interesting work done by
the unions when they are not going on strike, or 'taking over
the country' or 'holding the country to ransom'. However, it
also means that trade union news is likely to be covered if it is
'dressed up' in a manner which conforms to the media consensus view of what is a good story. This may involve the unions
using the techniques of the media in the way in which they are
often used with the unions, for example by learning the 'tricks'
involved in interviewing, arranging news or 'newsworthy'
situations. This has implications for the whole question of
'news management', some of which may be disturbing. It is
disturbing for example, that producers of news and potential
sources of news should come to collude in the stereotyping of
information in crude news models because there are few other
ways of access. This however, may be the result of the un-
spoken consensus underlying the news about the established
order of society. An elaboration of this process may be seen in
the journalist's concern for 'exclusive' stories: a story which
might get little general coverage is given considerable coverage
by one newspaper if the journalist is convinced that he has an
'exclusive'. This is not to say that any old nonsense will be
published on this basis, but it is true that a document, an action or a view has an enhanced news value if it is 'exclusive' to
one newspaper. Government and management sources are ex-
pert at arranging this and the unions are increasingly playing
similar games. This does not mean that access has become
easier or fairer: it means that news management has become
more sophisticated. 'Hard facts' are less important than the
tip-off, as of course they always have been. The point is
laboured because it is otherwise specious, in this context, to
talk about the objectivity of news or the neutrality of the 'hard
fact'.

Trade unions might be criticised for their laxness in supplying and checking television coverage of industrial affairs and
in paying too little attention to broadcast coverage compared

with that of the Press. Journalists may often show a similar lack of enthusiasm for the unions. In a study of the television newsroom, the Glasgow University Media Group says:

> None of them [the reporters] wanted to be an industrial correspondent when they grew up and liked least of all working as a reporter for this desk. 'Nobody likes being a runner for the industrial correspondent.' 'Who wants to go to boring T.U.C. press conferences or Barrow in Furness?' They complained of the 'caginess' of trade union interviewees, the routine replies they were likely to receive from them, and the whole cautious approach of industrial representatives, both T.U.C. and C.B.I., to interview situations. (*Bad News*, Glasgow University Media Group, Routledge and Kegan Paul, 1976, p. 176)

This latter criticism can probably be substantiated. It has of course to be seen in the context of the raw deal which trade unionists feel they get from the media.

It would be wrong to suggest that deliberate bias on the part of the individual journalist is the cause of the problem. The context in which the journalist operates and the hectic way in which what constitutes the 'news' is decided, militate against the most balanced and coherent way of presenting things that go on in the world. Many of the industrial correspondents are intelligent and sensitive journalists whose own integrity is not in doubt and whose personal efforts to present events in a straightforward and unbiased way may come to grief in the context of the leader, the feature, the 'colour' column and the selection of items actually printed.

The point can be illustrated by the *Daily Mail* 'campaign' in 1975 against 'extravagance' on local government, during the course of which it pandered in an exaggerated manner to popular prejudice about staffing levels and conditions in local authorities (obviously, for circulation reasons). The right of the *Daily Mail* to campaign on this question was not in doubt; it would be wrong to say that newspapers must not campaign. But the campaigning should not involve the partisan selection and slanting of news stories, the blurring of fact and opinion which newspapers claim to be at pains to separate. In this case, NALGO's concern was that the full story was not given. The newspaper failed seriously to explain the real cause of the financial difficulties facing local authorities and did not allow adequate space for replies by the union to exaggerated criticisms, although such examples of 'white elephant' spending that did exist were not condoned by NALGO. Facts about staffing levels, pay levels, overtime, stress and the serious impact on services were given repeatedly to the *Daily Mail* in conversations with reporters (some of whom professed themselves unhappy with their newspaper's own particular line in 'extravagance'). There was usually little chance of this information appearing in the news stories, however, and the union more commonly had to rely on letters to the editor to make its point. However, many letters from union branches or headquarters were either not published or were cut without consultation.

This kind of issue is, of course, relevant to the whole question of the concentration of newspaper ownership and the effect that this has on the kind of newspapers produced and the view of the world presented. Politically speaking, the great majority of the British Press is pro-Conservative, either explicitly or by virtue of belonging to a publishing group which has a pro-Conservative line. The rest is 'independent'; very few newspapers take a pro-Labour line. Newspaper owners have a right to support any party they wish but the marked imbalance in the Press gives cause for concern, and the possibility of launching new, viable publications on the market is small.

In 1975, NALGO published its evidence to the Royal Commission on the Press. It proposed, among other things, the public ownership of expensive plant, building and machinery, the setting up of an Independent Press Authority to grant franchises to groups showing themselves competent to produce newspapers, the setting up of a Press Council with real powers and the separation of advertising from circulation revenue. The aim was to encourage the growth of many different kinds of newspapers, representing all views, and to liberate, rather than to restrict, the operation of newspapers. A wider choice was to be provided and a fairer coverage of news given and the union argued that only fundamental reform of the system of finance would achieve this. Its proposals are worthy of serious debate.

6

Working for Television – the Experience of Censorship and Control

ANDREW GOODMAN
Freelance Producer in Radio and Television

Why are so few programmes that can be called, even in a vague sense, socialist broadcast on British television or radio? Perhaps the best way to answer this question is to follow the career of a hypothetical person, with strong socialist principles, trying to get a job producing programmes for B.B.C. T.V. Most of what follows would apply to working for the I.T.V. programme companies, or for radio. I have concentrated on the B.B.C. and television because it is where the bulk of my personal experience lies, and where the structure and the limitations of British broadcasting can be seen at their starkest.

The first area of control is, of course, recruitment. Our hypothetical socialist might find it hard to get a job in the B.B.C. at all. Working for the B.B.C. is still considered a privilege in many circles, rather like being called to the Bar or becoming a doctor. Even secretarial jobs are thought by many outsiders to be intrinsically more glamorous than similar jobs in business or the Civil Service. So the Corporation can afford to be very choosy about whom it employs.

The vast majority of people working for the B.B.C. (a number between 20,000-25,000 depending on whether or not you include people on short-term contracts) never have more than a nominal say in programme content. Quite apart from cleaners, catering staff and others who keep the fabric of the enormous organisation and its resources going, the average member of a film crew or vision mixer would only be consulted about what goes into a programme when it is a matter of taking technical advice ('Do you think we could cut better from Camera 2 to 3 if 3 was a little tighter?') or if the producer or director is either very thoughtful or very charming. Less than a tenth of the people currently employed by the B.B.C. have any real say in programme content.

Despite the prestige (which until recently was accompanied by low wages), getting a job in the B.B.C. is not enough in itself for you to be allowed to have a hand in programme making. People in technical grades have frequently been waiting years, even decades, for promotion to production departments. Sometimes the most talented are not promoted; this may be because their talents are thought more valuable (say as a cameraman) in an area where they are known, than in one where they are not. Sometimes one suspects it is because of their political views. Nowadays, if you wish to be promoted it is wise to play it safe; and playing it safe would include not being too active in your union.

Most programmes employ researchers; some freelance or on short-term (for example nine month) contract, many on staff. In the past most researchers have been women. To the outsider they may appear to be part of the production team; and indeed in some cases they are allowed considerable influence on programmes. But by and large they are supplying information rather than opinions. Our socialist could, if he or she had a university degree, enter the Corporation by this method, but it would be most unlikely that he or she would have much say in what programmes were made until (if ever) promoted out of this grade. The system of short-term contracting, too, means that the researcher can lack any security to show his or her radical opinions too openly.

There is no direct route to becoming a producer or director. When I joined the B.B.C. in 1966, I was chosen as a graduate management trainee. Mostly these came from Oxford or Cambridge, and there were about five hundred applicants for five or six jobs. The scheme was abandoned when the television service ceased to expand at the beginning of the seventies; increasingly the trainees seemed to be regarded by management as a source of trouble. One Conservative M.P. even alleged that one year's intake was dominated by 'Trotskyists'. The one such 'Trotskyist' left in the Corporation's employ today is not in the habit of producing revolutionary television programmes. The others have left out of frustration – and one was sacked.

This raises the delicate subject of political blacking. It is known that the B.B.C. refers the files of candidates for production jobs to the Special Branch for vetting. There is a conflict of evidence about what happens if the Special Branch says 'no'. Sir Hugh Greene, Director General during those *That Was the Week That Was* days of the sixties says: 'One thing I can state quite categorically is that there has never been any victimisation of anyone for their political views in the B.B.C.' (*Sunday Times*, 20 February 1977). Yet in the same article drama director John Nelson Burton alleges, with considerable evidence, that he has been consistently victimised by the B.B.C. for his politics for the past twenty years. Burton is the first person who thinks they are on a black-list to say so in the open; I could immediately name a dozen other people who in private claim to be on this list. The Association of Cinematograph Television and Allied Technicians (A.C.T.T.) has just set up a committee to collate these cases.

Television is a highly competitive profession. Even in boom years there is always someone else who can do the job, so black-listing is something extremely hard to prove. Management can simply turn round and mutter something about sour grapes. And it may not be purely a matter of political *views*. In my own case, I have seen internal B.B.C. memos which allege certain actions on my part. As I shouldn't have seen the memos, I can hardly put my side of the case. But leaving all this aside, I suspect that the B.B.C. management rather like people being paranoid about a black-list. Many inside the B.B.C., or some of those likely to get employment in production grades there, believe there is discrimination on political grounds. Naturally this may be inhibiting. Our hypothetical socialist, even presuming he or she reaches a position from which they can produce programmes, will feel there is a limit beyond which they cannot go. The recent dismissal of two assistants on the B.B.C.'s Portuguese radio service for alleged left-wing bias serves as a similar warning. This dismissal was, however, upheld as fair by an Industrial Tribunal.

If you are a socialist, wishing to produce programmes from

a working-class or revolutionary perspective, it is however unlikely that you will be sacked – unless you overstep a line
which is drawn for you very clearly when you begin working
for the Corporation. But your promotion may well be held up,
perhaps indefinitely, and your job may be made so frustrating
that you decide to leave of your own accord. You may not get
approval for your projects. In order to gain enough seniority to
make programmes yourself you may be forced to take a job in
a department which for some reason or another is considered
a backwater – such as the Natural History Unit or the Open
University.

But, suppose for a moment one manages to surmount these
obstacles and become a producer in a major programme area.
Could one make the programmes one wanted to?

It is not, as you might expect, as simple as that. For a start,
you would have to be a producer in the department best suited
to your ideas. It is no good working for Arts Features Department, for instance, and suggesting the idea of a film about the
real grievances of workers in British Leyland. One would have
to work in Current Affairs or News Department for that; in
these latter departments political control is tighter, and as
there is less time allowed to make programmes, films tend to
be more of a group effort. If someone does get the go-ahead for
a directly 'political' film in another department, as sometimes
does happen, a careful and particularly critical eye is kept on
the project by the Editor, News and Current Affairs – who is
in turn directly responsible to the Director General.

But on the whole, in Arts Features one has to limit oneself
to proposing ideas for projects which, however obliquely, deal
with 'Art'. This gives plenty of scope to the ingenious, but
does not make for direct, unequivocal statements about
British working-class life.

Even if you are in the right department there are further
problems. Even a fully fledged producer, with a salary of
£7,000 or more, is not in a position to deal directly with the
top level of the programme management – the programme
controllers of B.B.C. 1 or B.B.C. 2. These in turn are several
rungs below the Central Board of Governors: in this connection, the B.B.C. is far more hierarchical than the I.T.V. companies. Between a producer and a programme controller there

intervenes a head of department and very often a series editor as well.

Today B.B.C. television is programmed almost entirely in series or 'strands'. Only a General Election, the Olympic Games or Christmas cut across hour-by-hour, week-by-week scheduling; the schedules are usually adjusted only every three months. A producer must find an idea that will sustain a series of at least thirteen programmes, to the satisfaction of the Controller of one of the channels. And furthermore unless that producer has sufficient seniority to command the resources, it is necessary for one to find a 'strand' – be it *Panorama, Play for Today, Inside Story*, or a more *ad hoc* series – in which to fit one's ideas. That series has to be run by one's own department, except in unusual circumstances. The *Tuesday Documentary* is the only current example of a series accepting programmes from more or less any department; the tendency is to award the available 'slots' to senior producers with safe projects.

This need to fit into a strand is extremely inhibiting. As radicals are seldom in a majority in a department, it is our hypothetical socialist producer who will find him or herself in the minority being told that their style isn't right for the series. It is the radical who is forced into the role of being an individualist. Conformity becomes an extremely powerful pressure. But also, because of this long chain of command, pressure can be exerted from above in a number of subtle ways. A doubtful programme can be seen by the series editor, the head of the department, the head of the channel – and if it is sufficiently doubtful, by the editor of News and Current Affairs, the Director of Television Programmes, the Managing Director of Television, the Director General, the Board of Governors . . . with various other functionaries coming in on the act if they happen to be involved. 'Referring up' seldom, if ever, goes this far, if only because the lower executives know from previous experience what is and what is not acceptable. Only if they are in doubt as to the right decision do they refer to their superiors. But what prudent producer, of whatever persuasion, would not feel tempted to play it safe and so avoid all this fuss? If you fight every time, you become isolated from your colleagues and spend more time bickering with management than making programmes.

But it is the isolation from your fellow workers in production which is one of the most invidious forms of pressure. They feel they accept what you seem to reject: professionalism. One's peers as well as one's superiors in the command structure believe that there is a certain way of making programmes which is professional; there are technical standards for this (film that is shot in focus, comprehensible sound, and so on) which are largely unexceptional. But there are other standards which are no more than coded ways of disapproving of political content.

It is crucial to the working of a system like the B.B.C.'s that a programme maker is not openly accused of political bias very often, if ever. That would make a martyr of somebody, and perhaps give them too much self-confidence. It would also reveal how politically narrow the 'consensus' actually is.

I recently wrote the commentary for a B.B.C. *Omnibus* film about Portugal. The film making was described as 'naive' and 'unprofessional' by people in the B.B.C. The commentary was characterised as 'boring', 'obvious', like Dave Spart in *Private Eye* and so on. It was left to the people phoning the Television Centre Duty Office to say the film was 'Communist propaganda' ('and the best film [they had] ever seen on Portugal'). Under the guise of 'professionalism', these are essentially political criticisms. Strikes and industrial unrest, especially as told from the workers' point of view, are considered 'an instant switch off' by many senior T.V. executives. Apparently the ratings drop, and the executive producer can safely yawn, knowing there is no need to mount a serious political attack on the zealous radical producer.

What this all amounts to has been immortalised in the phrase of Huw Weldon, former Managing Director of B.B.C. T.V.: the 'pursuit of excellence'. Everything is judged by 'professionalism'. And 'giving both points of view' (even if one of these happens to be the status quo or a particularly exploitative multinational) is part of the professionalism. Baldly, making programmes which commit themselves to a socialist view of the world is not professional. In Huw Weldon's world, all good television aspires to the condition of a university debating society.

This is most clearly stated in the doctrine of 'balance' so

beloved of British Broadcasting executives and legislators. I once jokingly said that if the B.B.C. made a film about Auschwitz, the producer would be prevailed upon to include a reference to the population problem in Germany at the time. Two years later I was involved in the production of a film which dealt tangentially with the colonial history of New Zealand. The producer and I were talking about an incident where the British, having converted the native Maoris to Christianity, attacked them while they were worshipping one Sunday, and so won a victory they had been denied by more direct methods. 'But', one of our bosses quickly put in, 'remember the Maoris were cannibals.' By this method the B.B.C. hoped to produce a 'balanced' history of imperialism.

In this way there is a direct and overt intervention from above in the production of programmes. Current affairs shows like *Tonight* or *Nationwide* keep a log to make sure that an equal number of Labour and Conservative M.P.s appear over a given period, but both parties' constituents are rarely given such an opportunity. Balance also means that if allegation of fraud or mischief is made in any programme, a chance has to be given to the alleged mischief-maker to rebut the charge.

In principle, this may seem fair to a degree. But, as any monitoring exercise of broadcasting in this country has shown, this principle is not maintained as far as workers are concerned. The balance is between the powerful. What is important in this context is that most people who work for T.V. Current Affairs programmes *believe* they are being fair. They are very hurt if you accuse them of being 'anti-working class'. Because of all the factors I have mentioned the effect of this professional notion of balance is fairness only to the different sections of the bourgeoisie. On top of all this there are, from time to time, examples of direct censorship. One such instance occurred at the beginning of this year, when Ian Macintyre, the head of B.B.C. Radio 4, postponed the broadcast of a planned programme involving lesbians in the *Is this your problem?* series on Sundays. The subject was thought unsuitable for Sunday listening.

The I.B.A. has also engaged in the censoring of radical programmes. By contrast it has never revoked a commercial television contractor's licence, despite numerous occasions of companies not fulfilling the promises made by them in their bids for the available franchises. It has not made public efforts to stop commercial radio stations from apparently avoiding implementing the spirit, if not the letter, of the Independent Broadcasting Act. But it has quite often stopped the transmission of 'controversial' programmes. Several *World in Action* programmes have been censored in this way, but the suppression of the repeat showing of the *Viewpoint* series last year is the most ironic example to date. *Viewpoint* was a series designed for schools broadcasting. Its intention was to show, in the words of one of the series' producers, that all media messages are so removed from reality that 'it is ludicrous to claim that they *can* present a neutral, comprehensive, God's eye view of any situation. They are all interpretations.' She specifically included *Viewpoint* itself as being biased; the series was not a plea for a new kind of objectivity but a statement that all programmes are necessarily subjective. The series argued that the present subjectivities uphold the values of society. In the first programme it was shown that mass communications in Britain foster a narrow range of values and beliefs which form the received views of our society at the present time. The eighth programme in the series documented how political and financial pressure can influence the range and content of messages selected for mass production. One of the examples given was that of the Rank Organisation. According to the *Daily Telegraph*, Rank probably inspired the complaint about the programme from Southern Television (Rank owns one-third of Southern Television) which led the I.B.A., in May 1976, to ban a repeat of the *Viewpoint* series from the autumn schedules. The managing director of Southern, Frank Copplestone, complained in a confidential memo reported by the *Sunday Times* that *Viewpoint* was 'biased'. *Viewpoint* never claimed to be otherwise; unlike Southern Television and the I.B.A. The pressures pointed to in episode eight could not have been more graphically illustrated, than by the series' suppression.

However the most glaring and yet daily accepted example of direct political censorship in recent times in Britain is that of Northern Ireland; and here there is an army – police lobby pressing for *more* censorship of T.V. coverage (see, for example, the *Guardian* story, 15 March 1977; 'B.B.C. blamed for Police Killing'). As it is, very strict rules are adhered to, and there is a tight procedure of 'referring up' sensitive issues. Several documentaries about Northern Ireland have been made by B.B.C. or I.T.V. companies and then never transmitted. A similar if less spectacular watch is kept on other subjects; no local radio in the B.B.C. chain, for instance, is allowed to broadcast discussions on broadcasting. But my point is that on the whole, rules like this do not have to be made; most censorship is on the level of the subconscious.

This is particularly true in the areas away from news and current affairs programmes. As far as I am aware, a series about long distance lorry driving from the point of view of the drivers (rather than *The Brothers*) would not infringe the B.B.C. code of ethics. I do not think there would be anything in the B.B.C.'s code of practice that would eliminate the idea of portraying illegal immigrants as anything other than bandits, or stupid misled unfortunates. There is no need for such rules. The professionalism of any B.B.C. producer would usually make any such overt censorship unnecessary.

When Richard Cawston, the head of the Documentary Department at the B.B.C., finished his film about the Royal Family he showed it to the Queen. He was quoted in one newspaper as saying that Her Majesty had not asked for a single cut. To him this was proof there had been no censorship. To others it was an indication that the B.B.C. had chosen the right man to do a bland job.

But to return to our hypothetical socialist. By the time any would-be radicals in the B.B.C. are in a position to make programmes, they will have fought against the system, they would have compromised, had their promotion held up, and probably acquired a reputation among their colleagues as being 'wild', 'eccentric', 'difficult' or 'vague'. By this stage you are, as a sociologist would put it, thoroughly 'socialised'. You do not realise that you have become your own policeman; you do not notice that you are not suggesting ideas that would be automatically turned down. You do not notice that you always seek information from official sources and seldom from those affected by or participating in an action. You do not realise that you have forgotten to ask workers in a factory what they feel about their employer, or that when you interviewed the shop steward it was against the noise of machinery so he had to shout, while the boss was filmed sitting in his office. You still think of yourself as left wing, but you have lost touch with most of your real political contact outside of broadcasting. You do not realise that you have become part of the B.B.C.

There are exceptions; and I am not for one moment suggesting that it's impossible to fight these limitations from inside the Corporation. But most people who cannot accept the constraints leave the B.B.C. of their own accord; I know of very few who have actually been sacked. Some of us continue to work for the Corporation as freelancers, although outside the area of Drama, it is now very difficult to get freelance work whatever your politics. And as we have discussed already, there is the question of the black-list.

If there was a strong trade union organisation within the B.B.C. it would be very easy for black-listing to be questioned by employees and fellow trade unionists. There is no such organisation. The A.C.T.T. is not recognised by the B.B.C. although it has a high membership in some areas. The A.B.A.S., which grew out of the old Staff Association, is recognised, but is itself hierarchical in structure, with a constitution which allows little freedom for grass-roots initiative; its tradition is non-militant (though this has been contradicted by the recent practice of some of its members).

In my opinion it has a further and more fundamental weakness, which is in a sense the weakness of this chapter; the A.B.A.S. is organised on the basis of a different set of branches for production and technical workers. I mentioned at the beginning that technicians were in a vast majority in any broadcasting organisation; clearly their industrial power is far greater than producers. The terminology is inexact, because in television, production workers could not by themselves produce a T.V. programme. It is the continuing and unnecessary division between production and technical workers that is one of the principal reasons why there is so much indifference among technicians to the content of programmes. The division must be overcome within trade union organisations. In the A.C.T.T. (which has for a long time been discussing an amalgamation with the A.B.A.S.) workers are organised on a geographical basis; a group of workers for a company or building are organised into one shop. There are still substantial and fundamental divisions between technicians and the producer (many of the latter are not unionised in I.T.V., or are members of the N.U.J.), and concern for content is not paramount. But at least there is a basis of communication. Without this base, initiatives like the producer and journalist orientated Free Communications Group of the late sixties are likely to fail.

In 1976 the newly elected Government in Australia decided it was going to reduce the power of the Australian Broadcasting Commission (A.B.C.) the Australian equivalent of the B.B.C., although it is funded from taxation rather than a licence fee. The government thought the A.B.C. too left wing, and announced effective cuts in its budget and the appointment of someone very critical of the Commission as its chairman. This man, Sir Henry Bland, attempted to interfere with programme content. After protest from inside and outside the A.B.C. there was a twenty-four hour strike. In New South Wales, only tone was heard on all the A.B.C. radio stations, and only a test card was shown on A.B.C. T.V. The next day the A.B.C. workers (who incidentally appoint one commissioner to be their representative; currently he is a thirty-five year old pop radio producer) organised a mass lobby of Parliament in Canberra. By the end of the week the financial cuts had been withdrawn and a few weeks later Sir Henry Bland resigned.

The B.B.C.'s independence has never been threatened by government action of this sort. But it is worth noticing that no strike on any channel of radio or T.V. in this country has ever produced such a complete blackout, or had such devastatingly successful results. With the proper organisation and with the realisation by working-class people of just how badly treated they are by the media in Britain, industrial action could be this effective. And then, I think, we would find that a large number of workers in television production would see their role very differently. It would become a matter, not of individual, but collective socialist action.

7

Opening the Box – the Unions inside Television

ALAN SAPPER

General Secretary of the Association of Cinematograph Television and Allied Technicians

In 1970 the A.C.T.T. established a Television Commission composed of producers and technicians from amongst its membership to investigate the structure and operation of television in the United Kingdom. During the course of this extensive study – a kind of pre-Annan – the Commission prepared occasional papers on particular issues of importance. One such paper – 'One Week' – was a survey of television coverage of industrial affairs in the week of 8–14 January 1971. 'One Week' concluded that industrial relations were covered in 'a superficial and haphazard manner' and found many instances of scandalous partiality.

This study was a response to the television reporting of the power workers' dispute in 1970. That coverage had caused serious concern and raised for the union the question of how far television was able to deal with matters of social and political controversy in an impartial manner. Further concern had been aroused by new evidence produced by the Free Communications Group who had monitored the coverage of industrial demonstrations on 8 December that year. This pilot study also illustrated the high degree of bias in the reporting of industrial issues.

Following its publication, the in-depth study 'One Week' was accepted by the Union Conference and the union intensified its activity in this area. In particular, the Television Branch of the union was alerted to the increasing incidence of programme censorship by the B.B.C. and the I.B.A. and, from time to time, by individual commercial television companies.

It was noted that censorship operated at many levels. For instance, it was apparent that the censorship process involved an 'exclusion device' which meant that directors who were considered unsympathetic to promoting the *status quo* simply did not have their contracts renewed. Alternatively they were transferred to non-sensitive areas of programme making. An early example of this was the removal of a well known documentary director to the children's programming department and even to directing *The Epilogue*. This practice, of course, produced a situation where self-censorship became essential in the interests of survival. Self-censorship operates very effectively, particularly within the B.B.C. amongst permanent staff who know they would be at risk if they promoted programme subjects of a political content which were not in agreement with the established consensus.

Freelance directors and writers work at an even higher risk. Many of them are engaged on one-programme contracts or on a 'rolling contract' basis where the question of renewal is decided at the end of each three or six month period. From evidence gathered by the union it could be observed that individuals who had a political commitment which was not the same as the Corporation's did not have their contracts renewed and that their employment was markedly reduced. However, such a system did allow certain 'ultra-left' directors to operate where such political commitment produced an attack on all aspects of our society's structures condemning unions, union leadership, management and government equally. But overall, the in-built regulation of employment in the B.B.C. maintains in practical terms a biased stance against trade unions and the working class in general.

When the variety and range of programming was surveyed, it was readily perceived that it was not only News and Current Affairs but also entertainment programmes that reflected the corporate bias. One instance of management control was provided by the highly praised *Doomwatch* series which after a successful first showing was editorially neutered in the second series because of its high score rate against industry and government for their disregard of the human condition. Further, it was felt that the ubiquitous situation comedy caricatured its subjects to such an extent that a real and true representation of the life of the majority of the population was impossible.

Thus it would be wrong to imagine that bias against the unions is an isolated case. The bias spreads across all programming. When senior members of the broadcasting authorities are asked 'Where are the programmes on humanism? republicanism? atheism? or critical programmes on the armed services and police?', you are either received with blank amazement or referred to an insignificant 'quarter to midnight' time slot. Thus although bias is not produced simply by a secret cabal operating in the I.T.A. or B.B.C., it is the case that a dominant class ideology is maintained in part by the conscious and semi-conscious criteria used to select both non-fiction and fiction programmes. Broadcasting, in both its organisation and output, supports the property-owning class and its values. Capitalism may be allowed a few hiccups on T.V. but it must never be shown to be fundamentally sick.

This uncritical slant is itself maintained by the legal requirements of impartiality and balance. Impartiality, the clarion call and chief defence of the I.B.A. and B.B.C., imposes a spurious form of neutrality and balance on broadcasting which in a society characterised by gross inequalities can only be supportive of the social and economic imbalance.

On these questions, awareness amongst workers in the media developed to the extent that at the 1976 A.C.T.T. Conference, the following motion was carried:

Motion 11: Bias in the Media
This Conference deplores the misuse of the media, particularly press and television, to interfere and influence the democratic procedures of Trade Unions, in the interests of employers and anti-Trade Union forces.

It also deplores the continual bias in the reporting of Trade Union and industrial subjects (from which the A.C.T.T. itself suffered acutely during its industrial action of May 1975). This bias is not confined to home affairs. As an example, the Conservative bias in the coverage of Portugal led to the recent sackings of Antonio Cartaxo and

Jorge Ribiero from the B.B.C.'s External Services after 12 and 7 years' service, during which time their professional competence was unquestioned. They were sacked for alleged professional lapses. This Conference urges its fellow trade unionists in the A.B.A.S. to demand the reinstatement of these two journalists. This Conference urges the incoming General Council to set up immediately a sub-committee on bias in the media which will join with other media unions to develop a united strategy for action in an area which concerns us all and which will ensure that in future Trade Union and related matters get fair coverage.

During the early part of 1977, union branches were in the process of nominating delegates to enable the establishment of this sub-committee on bias in the media. In relation to the two Portuguese journalists, the issue was raised by A.C.T.T. representatives on the Federation of Broadcasting Unions. The B.B.C. Joint Shops Committee also protested. Letters and telegrams were sent to the appropriate broadcasting and government authorities.

Antonio Cartaxo and Jorge Ribiero, the two Portuguese journalists working for the B.B.C., had had the temerity actually to operate the impartiality often claimed by the B.B.C. They balanced the selection of news to reflect the actual situation in Portugal and not merely the interpretation in favour of the reactionary forces which had been broadcast week after week. These two journalists did not benefit from their union's support of them nor from their application to the industrial tribunal.

Meanwhile, the I.B.A. was busy taking extremely partial decisions on what programmes could or could not be transmitted by a commercial company. An education programme series called *Viewpoint*, which took as its subject the communications industry, was objected to on its first run by certain owners of a television company. The I.B.A. responded by cancelling the repeat showing. After a great deal of pressure from teachers and communications workers, they allowed a re-showing but excluded those sections of the series which were critical of Fleet Street. On another occasion parts of a programme which included Oxfam's campaign showing the disparity between the rich and poor nations was also banned. In the words of Lady Plowden, Chairman of the I.B.A., it was considered 'too political'. At the same time, when A.C.T.T.'s policy on apartheid in South Africa extended to the blacking of commercials covering South African goods and services, the I.T.C.A. and I.B.A. claimed they could not breach their 'impartial' role and still continued a policy of allowing such commercials.

An interesting case history concerning this author illustrates a type of distortion which is frequently in evidence within news reporting. During a television dispute in 1975, two individuals at an A.C.T.T. Northern shop meeting proposed the sacking of the General Secretary. This was leaked to the Press and later both in print and on television the story was expanded to the extent that the General Secretary was about to be dismissed for his handling of the dispute. After front page coverage in the national Press and full exposure on television, no denial was ever transmitted or printed. This experience reinforced the union's attitude to bias in the media and this was brought to the attention of trade unionists at large by the moving and adopting of the following motion at the T.U.C. Congress at Blackpool in 1975:

Motion: Countering Anti-Trade Union Bias in the Media
Recognising the over-simplification and distortion which characterises the manner in which the majority of the media discuss and report economic issues and aware that this over-simplification and distortion frequently expresses itself in savage attacks on the objectives and methods of trade unions engaged in free collective bargaining, Congress calls on the General Council to instigate the production on a regular and ongoing basis of a counter critique, deliberately written to correct and counteract the distortions of the media and to provide for shop floor trade unionists a straightforward and effective refutation of anti-trade union propaganda.

Congress believes that despite the useful contribution made by the publications of the Labour movement, the

T.U.C. must be more effective in answering the attacks of anti-trade unionists in the media.

Association of Cinematograph Television & Allied Technicians

This was followed at the 1976 Congress by the General Council's Report on the previous year's motion:

Countering Anti-Trade Union Bias in the Media

The 1975 Congress carried a resolution, 'Countering Anti-Trade Union Bias in the Media', which called for the 'production on a regular and ongoing basis' of effective refutation of anti-trade union propaganda and attacks of anti-trade unionists in the media. When the General Council considered this resolution they were informed that an examination had been made of the costs of maintaining a monitoring service of industrial coverage of television and that there was no reason to disagree with the estimates made in a very valuable study of this matter by NALGO and included a letter to the General Council dated July 13 which had proposed the establishment of a monitoring/research unit for the Trade Union movement. This had indicated that an initial cost for equipment might be £13,725 and an annual cost of £96,300 if undertaken on a full-time professional basis.

The General Council decided that as part of an examination of what was needed to offset anti-trade union bias in the media and as part of the process of achieving a reduction of such bias a special one–day conference should be organised. The programme for this would include, in addition to the presentation of the General Council's views and those of affiliated unions, speakers from television and the press. Arrangements will be made for the conference to take place after Congress.

Subsequently, the General Council of the T.U.C. called a 'Trade Unions and the Media' Conference which was addressed by Len Murray, T.U.C. General Secretary, who confirmed everybody's opinion by reiterating that the media certainly was biased against trade unionists. There were also apologetic addresses by representatives from the B.B.C. News and I.T.N. However, in the wide ranging debate during the course of the day, television and the Press were condemned for their arrogant and partial reporting of industrial relations news. A wide spectrum of representatives cited instances of the bias they had personally observed concerning their own industrial sectors. It was evident that the trade union movement as a whole had moved forward considerably not only to the identification of the bias that actually existed, but to a desire to do something positive to correct it.

The questions posed by members of the General Council and delegates were: 'Who selects the final news material? After all, I.T.N. and B.B.C. news receives far more visual material from their reporters than is actually transmitted. Which criteria are brought to bear on the selection?' In other words, 'who tells who what to select?' There were no real answers to these questions other than 'Well we are the professionals.' On the question concerning the criteria of selection we heard only the trite tautology 'That which is newsworthy.' The supplementary question, 'Newsworthy to whom?', was never answered.

During the discussions at the one-day conference on bias in the media, it was evident that the broadcasting authorities themselves considered that they actually observed their obligations to the public by maintaining a neutral position. Of course, one must remember how the B.B.C. defines 'neutrality'. Lord Reith, as Director General of the B.B.C. during the General Strike of 1926, gave the Corporation's definition in a famous letter to the Prime Minister, Stanley Baldwin:

> Assuming the B.B.C. is for the people and that the Government is for the people, it follows that the B.B.C. must be for the Government in this crisis too.

The fifty years since then have seen no substantial change in this attitude, when all strikes are considered damaging and all active trade unionists are considered as 'dangerous militants', 'mindless' or more recently 'unpatriotic'! The growing demand among trade unionists for definite action to redress the imbalance was expressed and indeed demanded at the Trades Union Congress and reiterated at the one-day conference.

It was proposed firstly that an archive of relevant news items and programmes be established. The I.B.A. and the B.B.C. keep sound tape recordings of news programmes but neither authority maintains to any great extent video or film archives of news of current affairs. Secondly, with or without such an archive in the hands of the broadcasters, an immediate independent monitoring system should be established. NALGO has already formulated plans for a monitoring system of its own and has urged the T.U.C. to adopt a similar system for the movement as a whole. At the very least a monitoring system could be established operated by retired trade unionists throughout the country who would receive a carefully composed code sheet to complete and return regularly to a central receiving and processing office. Thus a constant check on the nature and the occurrence of bias could be carried out. This information could form the necessary evidence to support the case against instances of imbalanced reporting or programming by broadcasters. The presentation of such evidence could be followed by a demand that instances of bias and partiality be rectified by retraction and further that alternative views be transmitted in an equally significant time slot.

There is no sympathy within the trade union movement for programmes censorship. The demand is for true equality of treatment. The final and continuing demand is for the T.U.C. to establish a standing Media or Communications Committee which would organise the establishment of an archive and a monitoring system and prepare case studies for representations to the broadcasting authorities.

Locked within the membership of the trade unions affiliated to the T.U.C. are thousands of professional experts in communications. The movement will have to learn quickly to call upon these invaluable resources to work for the benefit of not just trade unionists but indeed the community as a whole. The interest and responsibility of media workers has been aroused, not least by the arrogant actions of the owners and controllers of the television medium in which many of them work.

There is an increasing demand for consultation before a

programme is cancelled or neutered by editing out 'sensitive' areas. Members are demanding explanations both from the broadcasting authorities and from individual companies for alterations in announced schedules when pressure has been applied from industry or government. The activity of the trade unions in relation to this will undoubtedly develop in the immediate future. At present, it is apparent that those who own and control television also determine in a biased and unacceptable manner the content of the programmes they transmit. The trade union response must be to rectify this imbalance of power.

8

Beyond Monopoly: Mass Communications in an Age of Conglomerates

GRAHAM MURDOCK

PETER GOLDING

*Research Fellows, Centre for Mass Communications Research,
University of Leicester*

INTRODUCTION

The last nine months or so have seen a spate of official documents dealing with various aspects of the mass media in Britain. Last year we had the Interim Report of the Royal Commission on the Press and the report of the Prime Minister's working party on the film industry. The Annan Committee's enquiry into the future of broadcasting has just come out, and the final report of the Press Commission is due in a couple of months. In Britain at least, this degree of con- centrated governmental attention on questions of mass communications is pretty well unprecedented. Taken together these various reports present a massive amount of information and discussion of the present state of the British mass media, raising points that have not had much of an official airing before. On closer inspection however, their general framework of analysis turns out to be depressingly familiar and, we would argue, inadequate.

Reading through the various documents two things stand out. First, they all concentrate on the situation in one particular mass media sector and play down the importance of the inter-relations between sectors. True some of these links are mentioned in passing: both the Annan Committee and the working party on film consider the relations between the cinema and television industries. The Annan Committee also point briefly to the broader relations between broadcasting and other communications sectors such as the record industry. But by and large the terms of reference of the various bodies direct them to concentrate on particular sectors thereby preventing them from grasping the situation as a whole and making the question of the interconnections between sectors central to their discussions and analysis. What we have then are three self-contained bodies of enquiry, each investigating a major mass communications sector more or less in isolation from one another.

This fragmentation is reinforced still further by their failure systematically to relate questions of mass communications to more general areas of public policy. This is particularly unfortunate since the contemporary mass media occupy a central position in both the cultural and economic spheres. Not only are the mass media key distributors of the ideas and images through which people understand the structure and dynamics of contemporary societies and major providers of leisure and entertainment, but the scale of their operations in these fields places them among the leading industrial enterprises in the economy. Yet despite their obvious general economic and cultural importance, most discussions of the mass media tend to treat them as a more or less separate sphere, fenced off from wider considerations of economic and cultural policy. As we shall see later on, for example, the provisions of the National Enterprise Board explicitly exclude the possibility of bringing communications companies under the scheme. Similarly, throughout the so-called 'Great Debate' on education the mass media have hardly been mentioned. To take just one example, discussions of community education usually proceed with little or no reference to the parallel growth of community-based media facilities or to the possible interaction between the two. This separation of communications from other areas of public debate and policy formation serves to reproduce and reinforce the kind of fragmented, piecemeal and pragmatic approach to the situation which is so typical of the British system.

Our basic argument in this essay is that this piecemeal approach to analysis and policy has been overtaken and

rendered completely redundant by recent developments in the
structure of British capitalism, and more particularly by the
rise of communications conglomerates with significant
holdings in a whole range of information, entertainment and
leisure industries. It is now no longer a question of simple
market concentration where a handful of big firms dominate a
particular sector. Increasingly the leading companies have
branched out and acquired substantial stakes in several sectors at the same time. We have gone beyond the familiar situation of single sector monopolies and we are now entering the
era of the conglomerates. Faced with this situation we would
argue that there is an urgent need to move towards a more
comprehensive and holistic approach to mass media analysis
and policy. As yet however, most public discussions of mass
communications have not caught up with the growth of conglomerates. The general trend has of course been noted by a
number of people of widely differing opinions, ranging from
the Marxist cultural critic, Raymond Williams, to the ex-
Director of B.B.C. Television, Kenneth Adam (Raymond
Williams, 'Television and the Mandarins', *New Society*, vol. 39,
no. 756, 1977, pp. 651–2; Kenneth Adam, 'Britain's Broadcasting Future', *Gazette: International Journal of Mass Communication Studies,* vol. XXII (2) pp. 80–89). So far though,
commentators have not gone on to explore the extent and implications of the growth of conglomerates in any detail. This
essay attempts to make a start on this urgent task. More
specifically, it aims to do two things: (a) to outline the present
structure of the leading communications conglomerates and to
indicate the extent of their control over the major mass media
markets; (b) to consider briefly the implications of this situation for some of the major proposals for change currently under discussion.

THE RISE OF COMMUNICATIONS CONGLOMERATES

The last fifteen years or so have seen an important shift in the
structure of British capitalism, and indeed in the structure of
the advanced capitalist economies generally (see Derek F.
Channon, *The Strategy and Structure of Britain*, Macmillan, 1973;
and Gareth P. Dyas and Heinz T. Thanheiser, *The Emerging*

Enterprise, Macmillan, 1976). In contrast to the heyday of *laissez-faire* capitalism when most markets were characterised by competition between a number of small and medium-sized firms, the modern phase where most markets are dominated by a handful of large firms is often referred to as monopoly capitalism. Market concentration began in earnest in Britain in the closing two decades of the last century and has proceeded in bursts ever since. The last and biggest burst came in the 1960s with the spectacular boom in mergers and takeovers. In the ten years between 1957 and 1968 no less than 38 per cent of the companies quoted on the London Stock Exchange disappeared through merger (Leslie Hannah, 'Takeover bids in Britain before 1950: an exercise in business pre-history', *Business History*, vol. XVI no. 1, 1974, pp. 65–77). This movement produced a considerable increase in market concentration. According to one recent estimate, the average concentration ratio for industry as a whole increased from 57 per cent to 66 per cent in the period from 1958 to 1968. According to this calculation then, by 1968 the top five firms in the industrial sectors controlled, on average, two-thirds of the market (Kenneth George and Aubrey Silbertson, 'The causes and effects of Mergers', *Scottish Journal of Political Economy*, vol. XXII, no. 2 (1975) p. 125). The mass media industries were no exception, and as we have shown elsewhere, by the beginning of the 1970s the major media markets had concentration ratios at or above the average for industry as a whole (G. Murdock and P. Golding, 'Capitalism, communications and class relations', in James Curran *et al.*, *Mass Communication and Society*, Edward Arnold, 1977, pp. 12–43).

As well as a further consolidation of concentration in particular market sectors however, the last decade and a half has also seen another very significant trend – the emergence of conglomerates. Increasingly companies with a secure stake in one sector have begun to diversify their operations and to acquire interests in a range of other markets. The end product of this process is an amalgam of diverse interests which is usually called a conglomerate. Conglomeration has become increasingly characteristic of the leading firms in the economy, bringing with it a considerable increase in the reach and extent of their control over industry and commerce. Whereas in

1948 the top one hundred companies in the economy accounted for just under half (47 per cent) of the total net assets of industry and commerce, by 1968 their share had risen to 64 per cent (George and Silbertson, *Scottish Journal of Political Economy*, vol. XXII, pp. 179–93).

As with concentration, the media companies in the advanced capitalist economies have been caught up in this general movement towards diversification. Indeed, communications concerns have often been in the forefront of the shift to conglomeration. The giant American multi-media company C.B.S. is a good example. The company began in 1927 as a radio broadcasting service. Then, in 1938, they moved into records and are now the world's largest producer and distributor of recorded music. Next they acquired interests in commercial television, and currently control one of the top three television networks in America. Since 1964 they have diversified their interests still further, moving into toys, consumer electronics retailing, and magazine and book publishing, their best known acquisition in this area being Holt Rinehart and Winston. In 1975 their broadcasting interests contributed 36 per cent of total company sales, the record division 32 per cent and the publishing division 10 per cent, with the miscellaneous other activities making up the rest (C.B.S. Inc., *1975: Annual Report to Shareholders, of C.B.S. Inc.*, p. 6). As Table 8.1 shows, this pattern of conglomeration is also increasingly characteristic of the leading communications companies in Britain.

Table 8.1 shows the leading twelve commercial companies with substantial stakes in one or more of the main branches of mass media *production* – newspaper, magazine and book publishing; television programming; and the film and record industries. It excludes companies like Thorn and Philips who are concerned primarily with the manufacture of equipment, and companies like W. H. Smith which are concerned solely with distribution and retailing. All twelve of the companies listed in the table appear in *The Times* list of the top 350 industrial companies in the economy, ranked by turnover, and the first four in the table figure in the top 100 (*The Times 1000: Leading Companies in Britain and Overseas 1975-1976*, Times Books). In short communications is big business.

TABLE 8.1
Britain's top twelve communications companies

Company	Main sector of operations	Turnover		
		£ million	% accounted for by the main sector of operations	% derived from other communications and leisure interests
Reed International	Paper	1063	48	Printing/publishing 23
E.M.I.	Music industry	671	51	Electronics 31 · Television programming 6 · Films/entertainment 12
British Electric Traction	Transportation	437	30	Electronics/TV rental 28 · Publishing 3 · Television programming 7
Rank Organisation	Consumer electronics	353	30	Film industry 21 · Holidays 11
Thomson Organisation	Printing/publishing	236	57	Holidays 36
S. Pearson and Son	Industrial and commercial interests	230	52	Publishing 48
Decca	Industrial electronics	170	52	Music industry/consumer electronics 48

Granada Group	TV set rental 170	50	Television programming 24 Book publishing 4
News International	Printing/publishing 118	79	Paper 15
Associated Newspapers Group	Publishing 103	81	–
Beaverbrook Newspapers Group	Publishing 82	98	–
Associated Television Corporation	Television programming 71	43	Music industry 22 'Live' theatre 5 Film industry 15

NOTE: Figures are derived from the annual reports and accounts of the respective companies. The figures for Rank, Thomson, Pearson, and News International are based on returns for the financial year ending December 1975. All other figures are based on returns for financial years ending March–October 1976.

As Table 8.1 clearly shows, the majority of the leading communication companies are diversified conglomerates which
get anything from a half to two-thirds of their turnover from
activities other than their main sector of operations. E.M.I. for
example gets 51 per cent of its turnover from music division,
31 per cent from electronics manufacture, 12 per cent from
various film industries and 6 per cent from commercial television programming. The major exceptions to the general
pattern of conglomeration are the three newspaper companies
– Associated, Beaverbrook and News International.
Nevertheless, as we shall see, they do have important stakes in
other media sectors.

2 THE EXTENT OF CONGLOMERATE CONTROL

Having identified the leading communications companies, we
can now briefly examine the extent of their power. Exactly
how much of the major media markets do they control?

Table 8.1 includes all five of the country's leading
newspaper publishers (Reed International, News International, Beaverbrook, Associated, the Thomson Organisation) plus S. Pearson and Son, proprietors of the *Financial
Times*. According to the last estimate of the Press Council,
these six companies together accounted for 80 per cent of the
total circulation of all daily and Sunday newspapers, provin-
cials as well as dailies (Press Council, *21st Annual Report*, The
Press Council, 1974, pp. 116–19). Although a number of small
concerns continue to thrive in the weekly newspaper market,
here too the control of the top twelve is steadily increasing.
The leading concern in this sector is the Westminster Press, a
subsidiary of S. Pearson and Son. Associated Newspapers,
News International and the Thomson Organisation also have
significant stakes, as does British Electric Traction through its
subsidiaries, Argus Newspapers and London and Essex
Newspapers. Altogether the top twelve firms in Table 8.1 account for just under a quarter (24 per cent) of the total circulation of weekly newspapers (Press Council *21st Annual Report*,
pp. 120–23).

Table 8.1 also includes some of the country's most significant magazine publishers. The market leader here is Reed

International with seventy general interest magazines, sixty comics and publications for children and adolescents, and a hundred business and technical journals. Among the others, the most important in the magazine field are the Thomson Organisation and British Electric Traction. Thomson controls a string of important trade and industrial journals, and a number of successful general magazines including the *Illustrated London News*, and the high circulation consumer magazines *Living* and *Family Circle*, which are sold at supermarket check-out points. B.E.T. are also strongly represented in the trade and technical journals and through their polystyle subsidiary they have important stakes in the lucrative children's comic market.

Turning to books, the companies in Table 8.1 include a number of well-known names in the publishing world. The most significant is undoubtedly S. Pearson and Son. Their interests include the Longmans group, the Ladybird series of children's readers (which sold a record 25 million copies in 1975), and last but certainly not least, Penguin Books, the country's leading paperback house. The Granada Group are next in importance, with the hardback house of Hart Davis MacGibbon; Crosby Lockwood and Staples, the technical publishers; and the well-known Panther, Paladin and Mayflower paperback imprints. The Thomson Organisation also has an important representation in book publishing with the hardback imprints of Thomas Nelson, Michael Joseph and Hamish Hamilton, and the Sphere paperback house. Market shares for book publishing are notoriously difficult to calculate, but one recent estimate put Pearson, Granada and Thomson's combined share of the all-important paperback market at just over one third (36 per cent).

The 'Top Twelve' communications companies also maintain a very significant presence in commercial television programming. Three of the five crucial network companies serving the major population areas are owned outright by companies in Table 8.1. Granada Television, which serves Lancashire and the North West, is a subsidiary of the Granada Group; A.T.V. Network, the Midlands company, is owned by Associated Television Corporation; and Thames Television, which broadcasts in London on weekdays, is jointly owned by E.M.I. and British Electric Traction, E.M.I. holding 50.01 per cent of the voting shares and B.E.T. 49.99 per cent. In addition, another one of the top twelve companies, News International, is the largest shareholder in London Weekend Television, one of the other two network companies, with 9.6 per cent of the voting shares and 39.8 per cent of the non-voting shares. The leading communications companies also have significant stakes in several of the major regional television companies. The ownership of Southern Television, the station for the southern English counties, is concentrated in the hands of two companies, the Rank Organisation with 37.6 per cent of the voting shares, and Associated Newspapers with 37.5 per cent. The other major 'Top Twelve' holding is the Thomson Organisation's 25 per cent stake in Scottish Television, which serves the Edinburgh and Glasgow conurbations. Taken together, companies in the 'Top Twelve' either own or have substantial holdings in commercial television companies reaching 70 per cent of the total audience.

Table 8.1 also includes two of the country's leading television set rental concerns – Granada and Rediffusion, which is a subsidiary of British Electric Traction. These firms are currently ranked second and third behind the market leader, Thorn Electrical Industries.

In line with their general policy of diversification, the leading communications companies have invested in the recently established local commercial radio stations. The largest single holding so far is News International's 45 per cent stake in Thames Valley Broadcasting at Reading. The other major press groups also have significant stakes. They include Associated Newspapers' 20 per cent holding in Swansea Sound and their 15.5 per cent in London Broadcasting; the Thomson Organisation's 11 per cent in Metropolitan Broadcasting at Newcastle; Beaverbrook's 10 per cent of Radio Clyde, and Reed International's 10 per cent stake in Plymouth Sound. The big electronic based communications companies also have significant interests in commercial radio. British Electric Traction holds 17.6 per cent of the ordinary shares in Capital Radio, the very successful London station, and E.M.I. has holdings in Radio Tees, Radio Orwell, Radio Victory and Thames Valley Broadcasting.

Table 8.1 includes three of the leading home-based forces in British film production and distribution – E.M.I., the Rank *Film* . Organisation and the Incorporated Television Company (I.T.C.), a subsidiary of the Associated Television Company. As well as producing films on their own account (recent examples include Jack Gold's First World War flying film, *Aces High*, and the film of the popular television series *The Sweeney*), E.M.I. is also involved in joint production arrangements with Columbia Pictures and has distribution arrangements with the Dino de Laurentis Corporation who produced the re-make of *King Kong*. The Rank Organisation's stake in the film industry is smaller but still significant. They continue to operate an important distribution wing and to participate in the financing of production. Unlike E.M.I. and Rank, who have long been firmly established in the feature film field, the third company, I.T.C., has only entered the market in the last couple of years. Previously they were concerned primarily with making films and series for television distribution. Their products include such well-known series as *The Protectors*, *The Persuaders* and *Space 1999*. While they still continue with this they have now expanded into feature films with productions like *The Return of the Pink Panther* and *The Eagle Has Landed*. To consolidate their stake in the film industry still further they have recently added an exhibition wing to their production and distribution operations, through their partnership with the General Cinema Corporation of Boston, the world's largest cinema circuit.

Cinema exhibition in Britain continues to be dominated by E.M.I. and the Rank Organisation. According to one recent estimate, taken together they owned around a third of the total cinema seats in the country and accounted for just over a half of the box office takings. The Granada Group also has a small cinema circuit. It currently has twenty-six screens to E.M.I.'s 284.

In common with the British film industry, the British record industry has traditionally been dominated by two companies – in this case E.M.I. and Decca. Over the last dozen years however, this duopoly has been steadily eroded by the incursion of the giant American companies like C.B.S. into the English market, and by the rise of cut price L.P.s distributed by marketing organisations like Ronco and K–Tel. Even so, the two companies retain a significant presence in the market. E.M.I. remains both the country's leading record company and the dominant force in music publishing, although Decca have been somewhat less successful in combating the new competition. Even so, E.M.I. and Decca together continue to account for around a third of the market for both singles and L.P.s. Once again, as with the film industry, one of the most significant new forces in the market has been Associated Television. Their music interests have expanded rapidly and are now considerable. They include Pye records; Precision Tapes, one of the top companies in the rapidly expanding cassette and cartridge market; and a string of music publishing companies including the Beatle's old firm of Northern Songs, which together makes the group the second most significant force in music publishing after E.M.I. In addition, A.T.C. hold the U.K. franchise for Musak, the world's leading piped music concern. Other companies in the 'Top Twelve' also have stakes in the music business, although on a much smaller scale than the Big Three. British Electric Traction have a record and tape division, a music publishers, Lemmel Music, and the Ditchburn Organisation which provides background music. The Granada Group own a record company and Novello and Company Ltd, one of the country's oldest music publishers.

In addition to their holdings in the various mass communications sectors, a number of the companies in Table 8.1 also have interests in other areas of leisure and entertainment provision such as hotels and catering, holidays, bingo, sports facilities and theatre. Several of the 'Top Twelve' have stakes in the catering industry. E.M.I. owns the Angus Steak House Chain and the Royal London Hotel group, while Associated Newspapers have a controlling interest in the Pizzaland chain. Both the Granada Group and the Rank Organisation run catering and other facilities in motorway service areas. Indeed, Granada is currently the country's leading operator in this field. The Rank Organisation also have a very significant interest in the holiday business in the shape of the Butlin's Holiday Camp group. The other major 'Top Twelve' representation in this field is the Thomson Organisation's package tour operations.

In the overall provision of leisure and entertainment E.M.I. is far and away the most significant of the companies listed in Table 8.1. They operate over 150 Bingo clubs, run squash clubs, golf clubs, have a substantial interest in the Brighton Marina yachting and leisure complex, and operate the Blackpool Tower amusements and the Palace Theatre in the West End of London. Although out in front in terms of the scale of operations, E.M.I. is by no means the only member of the 'Top Twelve' to be involved in the general leisure and entertainment field. Both Granada and Rank run bingo clubs; British Electric Traction operate the Wembley Stadium complex which includes the Empire Stadium and the Empire Pool; S. Pearson and Son have Chessington Zoo; and the Associated Television Corporation own a number of West End theatres and have a controlling interest in the world's largest theatrical costumier, Berman and Nathans.

Even from the bald summary of the situation which we have space for here, it should be evident that the control which the leading conglomerates listed in Table 8.1 exercise over the major sectors of mass communications and over leisure and entertainment provision more generally is already very considerable. Moreover, it is increasing all the time.

IMPLICATIONS: SOME GENERAL PRINCIPLES

In the rest of this essay we wish briefly to examine various proposals which have been made to cope with the concentration in ownership and control we have outlined. We start from the premise that such concentration is unacceptable and that it poses a major threat to cultural democracy, for several reasons. First, concentration limits the range and diversity of views and opinions which are able to find public expression. More significantly it is those views and opinions representing the least powerful social groups which are systematically excluded by the process of concentration we have described. Second, concentration of control over the media into the hands of large conglomerates emphasises production for maximum profit at the necessary expense of other social goals that should be a vital aspect of communications media. Third, such concentration is undemocratic in two senses. It removes the media from public surveillance and accountability, that is it renders them externally undemocratic. In addition the concentration of control further away from the point of production reduces internal democracy within the media organisations themselves.

The objectives of organisational changes in the media should meet these dangers fully, and can only do so by resting on the preliminary assumption that the media are not just another industry, but an industry whose unusual capacity for universal social influence justifies extensive public intervention. In practice this axiom has never been denied; merely the degree to which it should be extended. From the licensing of book printers to legislative and fiscal controls of the Press, on to the more recent establishment of public broadcasting bodies, the media have always fallen under some degree of state supervision. In reviewing the various proposals under current discussion it will become apparent that the degree of such supervision remains the major area of underlying contention.

Briefly, we can set out the criteria against which models and reforms can be evaluated. These principles address the unacceptable consequences of concentration described earlier. The first such principle is diversity, the idea that the media should express or provide a platform for as full a range of views, opinions and forms of expression as practicable. Implicit in this is the notion that economic power should not be reproduced in cultural control; that the powerless should not be voiceless. Diversity is not, of course, guaranteed by multiplicity. Thus not all newspaper deaths are tragic losses, nor is a kaleidoscope array of specialist magazines a proof of diversity.

The second principle is that communications media should be accessible to all modes of expression, and all social groups with something to communicate. The principle of access is a necessary complement to that of diversity in confronting the problem of cultural restriction that economic concentration has created. Third, media need to be responsive to their audiences. It is a facile truism to repeat that communication is essentially two—way, but it is none the less essential that

economically powerful media are required in some way to
meet the needs and requirements of those who receive their
services. A fourth principle is that cultural production should
be separated from its finance. The production of mass communications primarily for profit, whether via the selling of the
medium's output to the largest audience, or via the renting of
audiences to advertisers, must distort the objective of diverse
and democratic communications. Fifth, standards of production, however defined, supervised or evaluated, must in at
least some sectors require large-scale production facilities.
Thus resources for such a scale of production must continue to
be available, though outside the control of the emerging media
conglomerates. The sixth principle is that of accountability, a
concern that has been at the heart of many of the debates
about the organisation of broadcasting, though less so in the
other media. At root this principle requires that the activities
of the media should receive, directly or indirectly, some kind
of public supervision; whether this is by the merest nod of
parliamentary approval or by the tightest ministerial scrutiny
and control remains to be argued.

A seventh principle to emerge from our characterisation of
the media industries is that communications media must be
considered *in toto*. What is, in principle, correct for broadcasting must be so for the Press. These various industries are
in practice no longer entirely distinct, and administrative or
constitutional discussions must reflect their consolidated
nature. Finally, external democracy must be complemented
by internal democracy. Those who work within the media
must continue to be the main force for their democratisation,
subject to the limits on their autonomy required by the principles of accessibility and responsiveness.

These principles are, of course, vague and incompletely
argued. They do, however, suggest the kinds of criteria by
which to assess any scheme which would attempt to deal with
the problems created by economic concentration in the mass
media, and the attendant development of diversification. We
can go on to look at some of these schemes.

PROPOSALS FOR CHANGE

In running briefly through the variety of organisational and economic changes that have been proposed for the media we wish merely to measure them against the criteria just outlined. There is no space here for a full review of such proposals.

The least revolutionary of the various schemes entail some increase in public supervision of the media. Their aim is to extend the accountability of the media, usually by strengthening existing supervisory bodies or inserting new ones. The functions of such supervisory bodies range from the arbitration of complaints, as conducted by the Press Council, to the ownership and allocation of communications facilities as now controlled by the Independent Broadcasting Authority. The first aim of improving such bodies has been to enlarge their powers. The Press Council is commonly accused, for example, of 'lacking teeth'. Since it appears to offer little more than admonitory finger-wagging it is claimed it could be more effective if more powerful. The problem of course is that such power requires the backing of effective sanctions, which would transform these supervisory bodies into something else, a step which proponents of giving them teeth seldom wish to take.

A second reform would incorporate into a single body a variety of disparate organisations presently involved in a single medium. The Prime Minister's Working Party on the Film Industry, for example, suggested creating a British Film Authority to incorporate the various cinematic functions scattered through the Department of Trade, the Department of Education and Science, and elsewhere (Prime Minister's Working Party, *Future of the British Film Industry*, H.M.S.O., Cmnd. 6372, pp. 28–30). Broadcasting has attracted the largest variety of such proposals. Raymond Williams has argued for a Broadcasting and Television Council (R. Williams, *Communications*, 3rd ed., Penguin Books, 1976, p. 167), the Labour Party has suggested a Public Broadcasting Commission (Labour Party, *The People and the Media*, The Labour Party, 1974 p. 13). Such bodies would control the allocation of broadcasting facilities and receive representations from the public. One of the more eccentric of such plans is the Annan Committee's idea of a Public Enquiry

Board for Broadcasting, which would hold hearings every seven years to allow public discussion of the work of broadcasting authorities (Annan, *Report of the Committee on the Future of Broadcasting*, H.M.S.O., Cmnd. 6753, 1977 pp. 64–70). Proposals like these rarely suggest such bodies should act without other more executive or powerful agencies of public policy. But they all fail to take account of the changed economics of communications, especially the rise of the multi-media conglomerates, and they therefore reproduce the fragmentation that bedevils existing arrangements.

To counter this, several schemes of public supervision have recommended a Communications Council or even a Ministry of Communications. A Communications Council was proposed in the Labour Party discussion paper 'The People and the Media'. This Council would have two functions; that of keeping the media under permanent review, and acting as an Ombudsman to receive and investigate complaints. The alternative idea, of a Ministry in which would be consolidated responsibility for all the arts and communications, has been suggested by among others a Labour Party discussion document on the arts, which was, however, unsure about including the Press (Labour Party, *The Arts: A Discussion Document for the Labour Movement*, The Labour Party, 1975, p. 24). The usual concern about such a Ministry is the stifling increase in bureaucracy it would generate. In addition it is feared it would centralise government control over culture in a potentially sinister way.

Both concepts of a Council or a Ministry usefully recognise the interlinking of the various communications media. The dilemma is that if on the one hand they were to be relatively powerless to prevent too centralised a control over communications, they would fail to meet the need for which they were created. On the other hand too powerful a body would raise the central issue of public accountability. This raises issues of the process of democracy which would have to be met in any event. There seems little doubt however that some overall policy for communications must be sought to cope with the problems we outlined earlier.

The second general way in which solutions have been sought is by public intervention in the market for media products. In the first instance this would be a trust-busting operation, requiring the larger groups to divest some of their holdings, and preventing the further consolidation of monopoly ownership. Existing monopoly legislation already deals with the media as a special case, though for some reason only newspapers are explicitly managed in this way. Since 1973 the Monopolies and Mergers Commission has operated within the Office for Fair Trading, and the earlier legislation was simply incorporated into the Fair Trading Act 1973. Part five of the new Act prevents any takeover of a newspaper which would result in a paper of over 500,000 circulation acquiring more than 25 per cent of another title, without the consent of the Secretary of State. The declared intent is to safeguard 'the need for accurate presentation of news and free expression of opinion' (Fair Trading Act 1973, para 59(3)). It is odd, therefore, that the passing of the new Act was not made an opportunity for other media to be included.

Monopoly considerations have continued to focus on the Press. A recent suggestion by Jeremy Tunstall is for a programme of trust-busting to be supervised by a new Independent Press Authority (J. Tunstall, *Will Fleet Street Survive Until 1984? – Evidence to the Royal Commission on the Press*, Dept. of Sociology: City University, mimeo, 1977, p. 42). The problem with any programme of divestiture is to decide just how much is required and how it is to be controlled. In addition the only bodies able to sustain the divested titles would be other substantial media enterprises, resulting in a redistribution of media power rather than its dilution. Professor Tunstall recognises this problem and suggests a complementary scheme of subsidy for new and weaker titles, supported by funds derived by the new authority from a levy on excess profits (ibid. p. 42).

The notion of a redistribution of funds from richer media to poorer is a recurrent aim of public intervention in media markets. 'Easy money' in the film industry is intended for such a use, and many of the schemes currently being aired for saving the Press have rested on such a basis. There is, not surprisingly, widespread opposition to such schemes from those media whose excess profits are in target. One major problem with such schemes however is their uncertainty. The monopoly or near monopoly structure of some media has evolved because of growing pressures of rising costs and falling profits. It seems unwise to base the economics of new or newly revived media on the unpredictable fortunes of those they are intended to succeed.

Public intervention in the market could take a more planned form via either direct subsidies or public investment. There are problems with both such ideas. Subsidies for ailing media may well keep alive unwanted media, as free market enthusiasts would argue. More importantly, subsidies, whether through differential subsidies of raw materials like newsprint, concessionary tax schemes, employment premiums or whatever, do not impinge on the internal decision-making of media companies. Their result is to secure the commercial viability but not necessarily either the social worth or public accountability of the media they help.

Predictably, suggestions of subsidy call forth stock responses about the degree of government intervention they would bring in their wake. The irony of this is highlighted in the immediate results of one subsidy scheme, that suggested by the Interim Report of the present Royal Commission on the Press (*Interim Report*, H.M.S.O., Cmnd. 6443, 1976). The intention was to supply public funds for Fleet Street to finance loans which would be used to introduce new machinery, and to meet redundancy payments in an effort to offload the excess labour in the industry. To avoid the accusation that strings of government control would be attached to the loan, the money was to come through Finance for Industry, a City lending consortium owned by the four big banks and the Bank of England. F.F.I. immediately warned that they would not provide the loans unless Fleet Street unions got a tighter grip on their members. Such was the disinterested alternative to state intervention.

Public investment, though usually attacked for being the thin edge of a socialist wedge, has not in practice led to public or governmental control. The National Film Finance Corporation spent many years stoking the dying embers of British Lion. After the Films Act of 1970 the Corporation was enjoined to act through a commercial consortium using cautious and highly circumscribed commercial criteria. By the end of 1975 it had only contributed to the finances of fifteen films (Prime Minister's Working Party, 1976, p. 17). The Prime Minister's Working Party report was more concerned to cream money from commercial television than to extend this uncertain level of government finance (ibid. p. 14).

Such problems suggest a third level of organisational form, that of public ownership of the media. Here the market would not only be corrected or adjusted by government intervention, but would be taken entirely out of the private sector. This would avoid the uncertainties of a subsidy system, while allowing ultimate control to rest with the origins of financial support. Public ownership could be either indirect, through a subsidiary board of some kind, or direct, as from a Ministry or Corporation.

One possible indirect form of public ownership could emerge from something like the National Enterprise Board, created by the Industry Act of 1975. The Board was intended to enter into planning agreements which would set out the strategic plans of the companies into which the Board invested public funds. Interestingly the Board is expressly forbidden from touching the media. Although never discussed either in Committee or in Parliament, a new section, 'The Board and the Media', was introduced after publication of the Bill, and voted in (with 66 M.P.s opposed) in July 1975 (*Hansard*, vol. 894, cols 1326–28). This prevents the Board from investing in newspapers or entering into any contract with the I.B.A. for the provision of programmes. Although in the event of 'serious commercial injury' the Board can be directed to invest in the media, it must withdraw from such activities as soon as possible. It would in any case be forbidden from controlling or influencing policy other than in financial or commercial matters (Industry Act, 1975, Section 9).

Other schemes have suggested a more direct public ownership of the media. This would involve either ownership of facilities, so that state-owned media would be publishing enterprises, open to production by others, or a complete state ownership of production, transmission and distribution. Raymond Williams has argued for something like the former in broadcasting, creating 'genuinely independent programme companies which will be leased all necessary production and

transmission facilities by an independent public authority'
(Williams, *Communications*, 1976, p. 165). The Association
for Cinematograph, Television and Allied Technicians
(A.C.T.T.) has argued for the complete nationalisation of the
film industry, right through production, distribution and exhibition (*Nationalising the Film Industry*, A.C.T.T., 1973,
passim).

Such schemes inevitably attract the stock response that
public ownership equals state control equals totalitarianism.
To meet this objection advocates of public ownership argue
the complementary case for workers' control within the
media, thus placing the emphasis on internal democracy and
the self-direction of those who produce mass communications.
The A.C.T.T. argue, for example, for a thoroughgoing system
of workers' control based on local work groups electing
representatives to management committees accountable to
those who elect them. Such schemes for workers' control raise
broader issues than the charges of impracticality which are
frequently laid against them. Even within a socialist strategy
for the media, they throw up more fundamental questions
than their proponents are sometimes willing to admit. It is to
such problems we turn in conclusion.

CONCLUSION: THE REFORM OR TRANSFORMATION OF
COMMUNICATIONS

The problems which arise in inventing schemes for the
reorganisation of communications revolve round three
debates. First there is the argument over the desirability and
degree of state intervention. Second there are questions of control and accountability. Third there are problems of access to
facilities. These are obviously related to each other, but for
purposes of this summary conclusion we can treat them
separately.

State Intervention

We are often assumed to live in a 'mixed' economy. But mass
media, like most industries, remain predominantly in private
hands. As we have described here and elsewhere these in-

dustries are in fact controlled by an increasingly concentrated group of conglomerates, whose diversified interests have largely avoided public scrutiny. This development has severely curtailed the range and variety of communications in a systematic way. *Private* enterprise in the media can thus in no sense be equated with *free* enterprise. Those who do make such an equation see state intervention in any sphere as creeping totalitarianism, or at least corporatism, and view it with particular concern in the field of communications.

The argument for state intervention rests on two points. First private control has not adequately catered for the democratic needs of audiences. The argument for consumer sovereignty claims that success in the market is the perfect index of audience demands, and thus the unbridled pursuit of profit is the most effective strategy for discovering and meeting these demands. If people wanted anything else, this argument continues, they would express their demand by paying for alternatives. If the alternatives do not exist it is because there is insufficient enterprise to provide them or because too few people want them by comparison with majority satisfaction with existing provision. Though superficially plausible this argument has two flaws. First the high cost of entry into contemporary media markets bars all but those already established (or, of increasing significance, those with significant financial power rooted outside the media). Second the economic logic by which media are forced to operate means that success (that is, survival), depends on catering for the largest possible audience or for the minorities that are attractive to advertisers. The structure of communications in the main thus comes to reproduce the existing distribution of wealth and power. The other plank in the case for state intervention is that communications are in some sense special. They represent a fundamental public utility comparable to health or education, and thus are too important to be left to the vagaries of the market. The Annan Committee, though concerned with the one medium which can claim to be used by virtually the whole population, none the less rejected the idea of broadcasting as 'an essential service' (Annan, *Report*, p. 132). The Committee is inconsistent on this; it elsewhere uses the idea that broadcasting is 'a scarce public asset' to justify increasing I.B.A.

rental charges (ibid. p. 178). Interestingly, however, the Sykes and Crawford committees (1923 and 1926) which ushered in British broadcasting, both stuck firm to the notion of broadcasting as a scarce public resource, to be used in the public interest under state control. There seems no reason not to extend this principle to all the media, for two reasons. First broadcasting is not uniquely scarce as a resource. We are not very far from having as few national newspapers as broadcasting channels; we have fewer major cinema exhibition chains than either. Second no medium can continue to be considered in isolation. The economic facts have overtaken this debate.

Arguing for public control raises, of course, the question of public finance. An essential service can claim finance from taxation. As such it must meet competitive demands from other services like health, education and social security. Other questions of priority also arise. What would be the priority between local and national media? How would news be produced? These and other questions remain after settling on the principle of public ownership.

Problems of Control

Public ownership means state control, and proponents of both must consider the administrative complexities that flow from such a transformation. The present models of nationalised industry are far from inspiring. The charges that are made against them of over-bureaucratisation, undemocratic centralised control, and management by appointees often unsympathetic to socialism or even nationalisation, are of course charges even more frequently true of private industry. None the less the problem remains of finding suitable models for public enterprise in communications. Raymond Williams has suggested a two-tier model for broadcasting akin to the finance and control of universities by the Universities Grants Commission (Williams, *Communications*, p. 174). The essential question is what kind of public accountability and democratic participation would result from these kinds of arrangements?

An essential contradiction arises in viewing workers' control as the solution to the dilemma of state control over com-

munications and their democratic structure. If communications are to be managed by those who work in the
media, what answerability do they have to their audiences or
to public bodies of supervision? Of course unions within
media are as capable of considering the public interest as
anyone else, and are more likely to do so than commercial
managers. But there may well be conflicts between the wishes
of media workers and their audiences which would have to be
solved by some other form of organisation than workplace
democracy. This conflict, it has been argued, would be resolved by the extension of access.

Problems of Access

The A.C.T.T. argue that access would dissolve the distinction
between professionals and non-professionals in communications (A.C.T.T., *Nationalising the Film Industry*, p. 30).
This of course raises a number of problems, not least of union
structure. For example, how would labour decasualisation be
reconciled with open access to non-union members? In addition many of the skills required in the media are more than a
compound of mystique and ideology. They are genuinely complex and inevitably specialised.

It is to meet these objections that schemes which conceive of
communications media as publishing rather than originat-
ing enterprises have been designed. Thus expertise and
technology would be made available to those with something
to communicate, whether as independent production teams of
professional entertainers, journalists or commentators, or as
private groups with a desire to be heard. The Annan Committee has proposed an Open Broadcasting Authority having
no editorial responsibility, but providing facilities for production and transmission by others. As they put it, the new
channel would be seen not 'merely as an addition to the
plurality of outlets, but as a force for plurality in a deeper
sense' (Annan, *Report*, p. 235). Others have argued that this
principle should be extended to a state publishing corporation, and so on. It is an essentially novel idea which merits at
least extended consideration.

A Question of Strategy

The various proposals available all converge around two demands. First they envisage increased public intervention and funding, and pose the question of whether communications should be extracted from the market system and evaluated by criteria quite alien to the basic values of capitalism. Second they envisage a shift from hierarchical control to democratic participation, that is an institutional as well as a financial transformation designed to increase the participation and power of producers and audiences. We are in basic agreement with both these demands. We would argue that many of the values they entail are currently available and that radical transformation and reform in the media are not irreconcilable. The B.B.C. may be bureaucratic, undemocratic and increasingly subject to pressures for demonstrable commercial success. But these characteristics do not follow logically from the principle of a public broadcasting corporation, and some variant of this principle is worth defending. Similarly for the Open Broadcasting Authority proposed by the Annan Commission to control a fourth television channel, dispute over detail should not condemn an innovatory principle.

The best strategy therefore is to defend those gains already in existence and to fight for those on the agenda. Making a virtue of disenchantment with the imperfections of existing arrangements will not hasten their radical transformation. The potency of even marginal shifts has often been indicated by the hysterical response they have frequently elicited from the present, commercial captains of media industries. This potency should not be neglected in aiming for a wholesale restructuring of communications within a socialist framework.

9

Bad News for Trade Unionists

PAUL WALTON

Senior Lecturer in Sociology, University of Glasgow

HOWARD DAVIS

Lecturer in Sociology, University of Kent

The findings on networked news output by the Glasgow Media Research Group . . . were strongly criticised by the broadcasters and we ourselves would not want to comment on the accuracy of the findings; but why do not the B.B.C. and I.B.A. themselves conduct such analyses?
Lord Annan's *Report of the Committee on the Future of Broadcasting*, H.M.S.O., 1977, p. 456.

Ever since the invention and development of the printing press by Gutenberg in 1457 mass media technology has played an increasingly important role in the development, form and struggle over ideas. The first mass use of any media technology was by Luther and his supporters in 1517. Luther's demands nailed up on the door of the Cathedral at Wittenberg were reproduced on posters and within weeks had appeared throughout Germany and France. By 1815 the power of the Press had become widely acknowledged among ruling elites; indeed Napoleon shrewdly suggested in his maxims that, 'Four hostile Newspapers are more to be feared than a thousand bayonets.'

The cultural lessons which flow from the history of media technology are very clear. The open flow of information, free communication has never appeared. Communication and the spread of information, especially current information such as news, has always been limited by the powerful: either to protect some existing *status quo* or for purely commercial considerations. The British state has been no exception to this rule, as any student of the mass media is aware. For example, following quickly upon the invention of the printing presses were the laws which restricted usage and readership. In England as early as 1543 there was an Act which forbade the reading of any English Bible by any man below the rank of Yeoman and all women other than those of noble or gentle rank. Similarly Raymond Williams has shown in his work (see especially R. Williams, *The Long Revolution*, Harmondsworth: Penguin Books, 1965) that the history of the establishment of newspapers was constantly restricted by licensing and tax Acts. For by 1762 the radical Press had arrived in the shape of Wilkes' paper *North Briton*. Following this and the emergence of the establishment Press, *The Times* in 1785, the government attempted to restrict the Press and throughout the 1780s and 1790s enforced stamp duties and advertising taxes effectively limiting readership and circulation by raising costs.

These historical examples are given here because many of the arguments used at present by the controllers and owners of what has been aptly called the 'Consciousness Industry' stress the technological or economic arguments against greater access or further democratisation. Other examples occur when we move from the past into the present and future. At this moment the British government – which is avowedly European in economic and political outlook – has done little if anything to bring us the point of view of other European broadcasters. We have in the skies several British communication satellites, most of which are capable of carrying up to six television channels in colour. It is therefore perfectly feasible to have a news channel added to our present channels which could simply consist of news exchanged between the European nations. Each country could swap news on an hour to hour basis. This is unlikely ever to happen, not for technological or cost reasons, for these would be minimal, but rather for reasons of ideological purity. West Germany's or Italy's coverage of events especially, say, in Northern Ireland, may well prove embarrassing. National rather than European cultural filters are still the order of the day.

The lesson for trade unionists in the study of mass communications is that 'knowledge is power'. Those who own, direct or control the means of communication are governed by the laws and conventions of nation-states, official secrets acts, libel laws and considerations of commercial and other interests. In this sense the notion of free communication obviously becomes an ideal to be aimed at; at present the free Press is a myth.

⌈Any glance at the major newspapers reveals a systematic and rather crude bias against the trade union movement. Strikes, if reported, are rarely given sympathetic or even reasonable treatment. Often their causes are totally ignored, whilst the possible consequences are magnified.⌐There is a sense in which much of this is predictable, for the Press has always been politically partisan. One can often gauge a person's politics from the daily paper they read. Moreover, the mass circulation dailies are all dependent upon commercial advertising from big business corporations and therefore it is unlikely that they would be critical of their paymasters. The circulations of the biggest four national dailies are shown in Table 9.1.

TABLE 9.1

Average daily circulation of biggest four national dailies

	1974	1976
Daily Mirror	3,968,000	3,864,000
Sun	3,446,000	3,521,000
Daily Express	2,822,000	2,668,000
Daily Mail	1,726,000	1,728,000

Between them the four sell around 12,000,000 of a total daily newspaper sale of about 14 million in the United Kingdom. Without advertising all of these papers would run at a loss. The revenue from advertising accounts for around one-third or more of total revenue depending upon the paper. For the local Press, it is even higher. In 1974, the last year for which figures are available, advertising accounted for over £68,000,000 of revenue for the four popular dailies plus the London evening papers. The so-called quality papers like *The Times* rely even more heavily upon advertisers. Faced with this fact, it is little wonder that the run of the mill papers do not support socialist or trade unionists. The total advertising revenue for national newspapers and Sundays excluding the local Press was over £166,000,000 in 1974 (all figures in this section are extracted from *Social Trends*, H.M.S.O. No. 7, 1976 and the *Interim Report of the Royal Commission on the Press*, H.M.S.O., March 1976). It is against this sort of background that the demand for a left-wing Press financed by the government has begun to emerge. The capital costs for an efficient Press are enormous, but then so is advertising expenditure. Indeed one of the prime reasons preventing the success of a left-wing Press is that advertising revenue would be minimal. It would therefore have to compete, hampered by fewer pages, selling at a higher price, produced with fewer staff – in short, if it avoids bankruptcy, it is probably doomed to sell only to the committed. If it does succeed, its circulation, like the *Morning Star* or other radical papers, will probably be small. Indeed it is sometimes necessary for these papers to maintain low circulations as they are printed and sold at a loss. A large print run could not be financed. A simple solution to this lack of alternatives in newspapers would be the introduction of a special advertising tax in the newspaper and print industry (see for example the T.U.C. proposals on the media, Appendix 1 and *The People and the Media*, the report of a Labour Party study group, 1974). They receive in excess of £200 million per year from advertisers. A tax of only ten pence in the pound on this source of revenue would raise over £20 million which could be used to finance alternative newspapers. Of course the immediate and likely response to such arguments is that this would constitute an infringement of the free Press. But the Press as we have shown is certainly not free. Aside from its other constraints, it is dependent for survival upon the big commercial advertisers – hardly an ideal situation for the free reporting of information.

As long ago as 1961 the Shawcross Commission warned of the dearth of alternative newspapers brought about by concentration of Press ownership and stated: 'The greater the number of newspapers which are governed by the same editorial policy the greater is the danger; the risk is yet more serious if any of the publications is associated in some way

TABLE 9.2
The interlocking ownership in the media

Major newspaper groups	*TV contractor or commercial radio company in which shares held*
Beaverbrook News-papers	Associated Television Corporation Capital Radio Radio Clyde
Reed International	Associated Television Corporation Radio Clyde
News International	London Weekend Television Birmingham Broadcasting
Associated Newspapers	Harlech Television Southern Television London Broadcasting Company
Thomson Organisation	Scottish Television
S. Pearson & Son	London Weekend Television
Daily Telegraph	London Weekend Television
Observer (Holdings)	London Weekend Television Capital Radio
Manchester Guardian & Evening News	Anglia Television Greater Manchester Independent Radio
United Newspapers	Trident Television Radio Hallam (Sheffield)
The Iliffe family	Associated Television Corporation Birmingham Broadcasting

with other potential influences such as television.' Yet this warning has been virtually ignored. Indeed interlocking ownership has meant that not only has there been a greater concentration of cultural power in the hands of the few big companies, but that the super profits made out of commercial television and radio can be used to support the predominantly right-wing national Press. Table 9.2, taken from Labour research in July of 1975, demonstrates how far this interlocking ownership pattern has gone.

Moreover, the profits expressed as a return on capital employed by these companies is extremely high. The I.B.A. reported that expressed in this fashion the return was 78.5 per cent in 1973 and even in 1974 it was 48.3 per cent. The I.B.A. also report that while the costs of the I.T.V. companies were £149.2 million in 1976 the income from advertising was £209.3 million. It is not surprising that commercial television has been described as a licence to print money. However it is not simply the commercial question which is at stake. Since the Pilkington Committee on television there have been legal requirements to reduce control of T.V. companies by newspaper companies, but the holdings are still massive. Lord Annan's Commission on the Future of Broadcasting notes that 'In Australia, newspaper interests have gained control of television stations with very sharp repercussions upon political expression and news.' The committee asked 'if there was a risk of the same thing happening here?' (Annan, *Report*, p. 198). They seem to feel that this is unlikely because contracts can be revoked. They recommend as a preventive measure that no newspaper has more than 10 per cent of the voting shares in any T.V. company. The problem is that less than 10 per cent of the voting shares in a large company can give effective control. For even 1 per cent of the voting shares of a large company may mean that the newspaper is the largest voting bloc. Moreover, in response to this the *Economist* produced a list of what it called the newspaper shares that may be hurt by this proposal (*Economist* 26 March 1977). The list reveals that six of the commercial T.V. companies are partly owned by newspaper companies. Five of these six own between 13.9 per cent and 37.5 per cent of the voting shares. As the *Economist* notes, 'if some of the newspapers had to reduce their television interests the effect on their profit and loss account would be considerable'. Perhaps this would not be such a bad thing, for at present the cultural climate is partly shaped by such ownership patterns. Trade unionists may well ask why right-wing newspapers should stagger along apparently existing on the returns from the super-profits and advertising revenue from television companies. The breaking up of such combines may well come to mean a better television service and a freer Press.

CULTURAL POWER

The danger in the kind of analysis offered above is that we come to concentrate on purely economic or commercial considerations. The importance of the mass media resides not merely in its commercial exploitation but in its general effects upon our ideas, attitudes, beliefs and actions. The 'Consciousness Industry' is an everyday business, and we are both subtly and crudely influenced by the Press and television output. Hans Magnus Enzensberger, a German cultural critic and poet, has argued that the 'mind industry' has become one of the key industries of the twentieth century. He believes that it has become central because the manipulation of consent and agreement is necessary in an advanced industrial society – which is rigidly hierarchical in rewards and dividends. But Enzensberger argues that the commercial exploitation of this area is incidental. The job of the mind or consciousness industry is to sell the myth that exploitation and inequality are vanishing. He argues that if you buy a book you pay costs and profit; if you buy a magazine or newspaper, you only pay a fraction of the costs; if you tune into radio or television your set is virtually free. Enzensberger's view is that the commercial exploitation of the media is not central and not intrinsic to it. According to him the consciousness industry's main business is to sell the 'existing order', to perpetrate the prevailing pattern of structural inequality and domination. Enzensberger's analysis of the structure of the media is distinguished by the fact that it concentrates upon exactly those issues which Marshall McLuhan, the American Media Guru, refuses to address – the political and social implications of the electronic media for the class structure of industrial societies.

From one perspective, Enzensberger is absolutely accurate, for the general output of the mass media is ideological; but it is not consciously so. Rather, the cultural assumptions of the dominant groups within our society are given privileged and central treatment. The media's messages are not neutral, although they may appear as such. Television is perhaps the best medium for examining the mediated representation of the culturally dominant forms of our society, for in the post-war period it has come into unchallenged dominance as the prime medium of entertainment and news communication. Most families spend between four and five hours per day watching the T.V. Just behind the drama, the serials, the comedy and the news lie the dominant messages we receive, encoded in routine and convention. It has become a matter of critical importance to monitor this output, to examine it and to try to control its constant flow. It was for these kind of reasons that the Glasgow Media Group chose to undertake a long scientific study of news output.

TELEVISION NEWS AND NEUTRAL FORM

In all of this one thing is clear – we believe there is no simple conspiracy at work. The media is too complex and media personnel too varied for the notion of a 'right-wing plot' or deliberate manipulation to hold water as a complete theory of how the media works. The production of television is itself an industrial process and an extremely sophisticated one at that. Like all such processes it has its own routine practices, preferences and normal working assumptions. These are not often discussed by workers inside the television industry any more than similar rules are discussed in other industries. Consideration of them seldom enters the debate about 'television bias'. We have been trying to establish what these 'rules' are, and we think we can begin to identify some patterns in the way they are usually applied. Without an understanding of these 'rules' the concept of bias will remain contentious and the possibility of improving coverage in one direction or another elusive.

Television news is one of our most important 'windows of the world' and at the same time a window which distorts our view of that world. News broadcasts on television reach a larger and more varied audience than any other news medium. For most people broadcasting is now the prime source of information in British society. The importance of television news does not only have to do with the amount of time we spend watching the box for the news occupies a special position in the flow of television output. We may sit down to watch an evening's television but we know when we

are watching a play, a quiz show, the news or a documentary.
We recognise the news because there are special rules and
conventions built into news production and presentation.
They derive partly from the B.B.C. Charter and the Independent Television Acts and partly from journalists' assumptions
about what news is.

Ostensibly the acts governing television news are strict. The
Minister responsible for broadcasting has required the B.B.C.
to refrain from expressing the opinions of the Corporation on
current affairs or on matters of public policy. The I.B.A. Act
of 1973 requires the I.B.A. to ensure that, all news given in the
programmes (in whatever form) is presented with due accuracy and impartiality and 'that due impartiality is preserv-
ed on the part of persons providing the programmes as
respects matters of political or industrial controversy or
relating to current public policy' (I.B.A. Act, 1973). It is this
legal obligation and the conventions surrounding it which
mean that broadcast news, in form at least, has to have the
veneer of neutrality and balance. As the television frequencies
have been handed to few companies, Parliament deliberately
restricted the broadcasters from disseminating their own
views on news and current affairs programmes. It is these
features which differentiate television news from the obviously
partisan Press. Unfortunately, with other factors, it has led a
large majority of people to assume the objectivity of the news
output. According to audience research most viewers accept
this authority. They believe that television news is the 'most
accurate and trustworthy source' of news. This is even true of
people who are more likely to listen to the radio or read a
newspaper to get the day's news.

Of course charges of bias have been levelled against the
news from politicians of all parties, from the C.B.I. and, not
least, from trade unionists. In 1971 the A.C.T.T. Television
Commission undertook a pioneering study of one week's
television news output and cast serious doubt on the claimed
impartiality of industrial reporting. More recently, we at the
Glasgow University Media Group have started a long-term
study of the ways in which television news currently fails to
achieve balance and impartiality in the coverage of industrial
affairs. In the first six months of 1975, the Group monitored,

videotaped and analysed every news bulletin on all three
channels. ⌡

EMPTYING THE BOX

The first task was to describe how the different items of news
are assembled every day into programmes which have the
same length, similar numbers of items and comparable types
of story in the same order – regardless of fluctuations of activity outside the newsroom. It appears that whatever happens in
the real world will be accommodated within a consistent
pattern which news personnel take for granted. So for the
viewer as well as the journalist, the amount of time devoted to
political or foreign stories (always much greater than the time
given to consumer or crime stories, for example) appears to be
quite 'natural'. This apparent naturalness is enhanced by the
extraordinary similarity between channels. It could be argued
that the same mix of stories on different channels simply
proves that the news is holding up a mirror to the same external reality. But this is not so. The images we see, the stories we
hear, are prefabricated according to internal, journalistic
criteria. It is as though the journalist has to fill in an outline
that has already been drawn and he or she already knows
what should go in before the 'news' has happened.

Within this apparently natural outline or framework, industrial news has an important place. It regularly takes up
about one-fifth of the bulletins. It is second only to political
and foreign stories in the amount of time devoted to it. In
terms of the organisation of the newsroom, industrial news is a
category of reporting which receives the special attentions of
Industrial Correspondents and Senior Editors. In television
news then, industrial affairs are not played down. They are, if
anything, underlined as being serious and newsworthy. But
what exactly do we receive when we hear an item being introduced with the words: 'And now some industrial news'?

MORE BAD NEWS FROM THE CAR INDUSTRY

In the first six months of 1975, half of all industrial stories in
the bulletins were concerned with just three industries –

transport and communication, public administration and, overwhelmingly, vehicle manufacture. This means that the 2.1 per cent of Britain's work force who make cars and other vehicles got 24.4 per cent of the television news' general industrial coverage.

The coverage of strikes reveals the same distortion. Shipbuilding and engineering, with a high incidence of strikes, received negligible coverage. Mining, construction and chemicals received no coverage at all. Of the twenty principal disputes (those singled out by the Department of Employment as being particularly significant for the economy), nine were not mentioned at all on television news. The average viewer must therefore suffer serious perceptual inaccuracies if he regards the industrial news as a guide to what is actually happening. This extraordinary propensity to report the car industry was the most noticeable of the distortions in the early months of 1975. But when particular stories are examined in detail, the tendency to present one side of a case rather than another becomes even clearer.

This is not to say that the news consciously and deliberately tries to load the case in one direction rather than another. In fact the Glasgow Group found that interviews were held with a wide range of spokesmen. What is interesting about who gets on is that what they have to say may be either given authority or be discredited by the context of the interview. This can be seen most obviously in the interviews with women. The B.B.C. seems to have slightly more interviews with women than I.T.N. Of the 843 named interviewees in the first three months of 1975, only 7.7 per cent were women. They were more likely to be interviewed in connection with disaster or sports stories than in industrial or economic stories. Moreover many women trade unionists have made the point to us that the news simply tends to assume that workers are men. Wives are rarely interviewed unless, as in the classic instance of some of the 'Cowley wives', they are actively against the dispute. A crude and typical example of this in news broadcasts is the assumption that workers are men. These two words are often used interchangeably in the news. The following *News at Ten* report on the Triumph Motor Cycle workers' co-operative provides a clear example of this.

Trevor McDonald reporting on the Meriden co-operative:

> The *workers'* co-operative at the Triumph Motor Cycle fac-
> tory in Meriden was born not out of trade union idealism
> but out of the determination of *the men* to save their jobs and
> the Triumph name . . . (I.T.N. *News at Ten* 13 May 1975)

Later in the same interview we learn in fact that:

> . . . with the exception of the Managing Director and the
> Company Secretary, all *the workers* earn a flat £50 a week.
> There is no payment for overtime. There are specialist jobs,
> but the non-specialist ones are shared. *Margaret Wright*
> assists in the final assembly of motor cycle petrol tanks and
> doubles up as telephone operator and receptionist as well.
> (I.T.N. *News at Ten* 13 May 1975)

However, it is not simply women workers who receive the
inaccuracies and imbalances which flow from the dominant
culture of our society. Although in the news as a whole there is
the semblance of balance between the 'two sides', they appear
in different contexts. Workers are more likely to be interviewed in groups, in the street, in noisy surroundings etc.,
while management are more likely to be filmed in surroundings which help to lend authority to their statements. In fact
the constant assumption that there are only two sides means
that whilst there is often formal balance between trade union
representation and that of management – if the strike is not an
official strike, and as many as 70 per cent are not – then the
shop floor view may not surface at all. Other routine features
of industrial news are the frequent omission of the cause of the
dispute, and the over-concentration on effects or consequences. There is the constant assumption of the correctness
of the managerial argument that strikes achieve nothing and
are therefore basically irrational. The news often fails to dis-
tinguish between official and unofficial disputes indicating
which unions or workers are involved. The assumption on the
economic news in the period the Glasgow Group studied was
more than likely to be that inflation is wages-led, and that all
major strikes are merely over pay. Workers tend to be

stereotypically filmed by the factory gates or on a picket line. They are rarely accorded a studio and almost never shot talking directly face on to camera – as those of 'higher' status are.

The industrial news thus provides us with an interesting case study of how the practice of the culture of television operates in an everyday fashion. The claims and conventions are that it is fair, impartial and balanced. In practice the imbalances vary from the crude assumptions and routines noted above to the more deeper cultural coding of camera angles or story routines.

TELLING STORIES

Stories are presented in ways which do let the facts speak for themselves but which represent one particular point of view – this in spite of the claim that news presents 'facts' neutrally and impartially.

The Glasgow dustcart drivers' strike was one of the biggest stories featured in the bulletins between January and April 1975. It was a dispute between the H.G.V. drivers (many of whom were drivers of dustcarts) and the Glasgow Corporation: troops were eventually called in by the Corporation to help clear uncollected refuse. The telling of the story in fact concentrated on the 'health hazard' issue, indeed long before enough refuse had piled up for it to become a serious health hazard. The point is not that the accumulation of rubbish was unnecessary, rather that it was emphasised to the exclusion of other central issues, such as the cause. In the 13 weeks of the strike, the causes of the strike were mentioned only 11 times out of 40 items on B.B.C. 1, 6 times out of 19 on B.B.C. 2 and 19 times out of 43 on I.T.N.

The Group's study of the British Leyland engine tuners' strike at Cowley in the same period shows a similar tendency. Here the Prime Minister's speech on 3 January 1975 referring to 'manifestly avoidable stoppages of production' caused by management *and* labour was transformed in twenty-nine later references to apply to the work force *alone*, and the view that 'the ills of British Leyland' could be laid substantially at the door of the labour force. As against B.B.C. 1's 22 references to Leyland's 'strike problem', there were 5 references to 'management failings' and 1 to the company's investment pattern. On B.B.C. 2 there were 8 references to strikes as against 3 to management and 2 to investment; on I.T.N. 33 to strikes, 8 to management and none to investment.

These persistent, one-sided interpretations of events reported constitute a 'dominant view' of the event. These dominant views are used to select which aspects of a situation shall be reported and which omitted. They operate within un-spoken sets of assumptions which match up with a basic view of our national life and the place of industry, government, un-ions and other institutions within it. They present a coherent, consensual and partisan view of the world which may have little to do with the personal opinions and beliefs of individual journalists, but which limits and defines what they can say. The use of particular dominant views means that bulletins ac-tually present explanations constantly and implicitly – even when they are not claiming to editorialise or comment but simply to present the 'facts'. What the research shows is that there are no 'unadorned facts' but that all news is refracted and shaped in the processes of its production.

WHO SAYS SO?

Like the bulletin profiles and the organisation of stories, the language of the news – its words and phrases, and the manner of their creation – is highly limited, convention-bound, restricted and formal. To say, for instance, that 'ambulance officers have begun their strike' or to use the phrase, 'the Cowley engine tuners' dispute' is to say more than that there is a dispute between two industrial groups. It is to label a com-plex event in a particular way. In television news our linguistic analysis reveals that the terms which are specific to action by labour (strike, work to contract) *as well as* those embracing both disputants (dispute, disruption) are applied solely to labour. The reporting is structured in a way which makes labour the active party of industrial disputes – the group which provokes or precipitates action and which, by implica-tion, is responsible. The effect of ignoring or obscuring the identity of the employer (firm, corporation or government) and giving a minimum of circumstantial detail is to allow

workers the dubious privilege of the appearance of a group of
people with apparently suspect motives precipitating action
against impersonal institutions and organisations whose
legitimacy is taken for granted. Thus we don't hear of
employers 'demanding' that labour agree to work harder or
unions 'offering' to accept more. As far as television news is
concerned, industrial news is generally bad news, or news of
'trouble'. This is synonymous with trouble 'caused by'
labour/strikes and hardly ever refers to trouble of another
kind – the difficulties arising from mismanagement or the
economic situation at large.

So, down to the finest details of language, the news speaks
from a position which is far removed from the interests of the
majority of those who work in industry and who are the subjects of those events which are reported in the industrial news.
In trying to adopt a 'detached view' it makes use of assumptions similar to those of the dominant commercial, financial
and political interests in our society. When these interests are
challenged, as they often are in the industrial sphere, the news
works to reinforce and uphold the dominant, conservative
social values. As such it is inimical to the interests of labour.

THE FUTURE OF BROADCASTING

The Parliamentary Commission on the future of broadcasting
under Lord Annan specifically mentions the failure of broadcasters to give adequate and proper thought to balanced
coverage in the industrial area. It states that 'the broadcasters
were not guilty of deliberate and calculated bias. But that the
coverage of industrial affairs is in some respects inadequate
and unsatisfactory is not in doubt' (Annan, *Report*, p. 272). In
short, much of the evidential claims that were made by the
Glasgow Group in the book *Bad News* (Routledge and Kegan
Paul, 1976) and to be further substantiated in the second
volume *More Bad News* have now been accepted by a
parliamentary commission, who noted that 'Difficult as the
reporting of industrial stories may be, the broadcasters have
not fully thought it through' (Annan, *Report,* p. 272). The
specific charges that Annan makes in this area of news broadcasters are that:

They too often forget that to represent the management at their desks, apparently the calm and collected representatives of order, and to represent shop stewards and picket lines stopping production, apparently the agents of disruption, gives a false picture of what strikes are about. The broadcasters have fallen into the professional error of putting compelling camera work before news. Furthermore the causes of why people come out on strike are often extraordinarily complex. No reporter does his job adequately if he interviews only the leading shop steward or union official. The fact that a strike is not backed by the union does not exonerate broadcasters from discovering why the work force is out. The Glasgow Media Group reported that in the unofficial Glasgow dustcart drivers' dispute in 1975, during 13 weeks and 21 interviews shown on the national news none of those on strike was interviewed. (Annan, *Report*, p. 272.)

The question that arises is what is to be done about such systematic distortions and absences. The Media Group has never rested its claim on the fact that such bias and lack of balance was generally intentional. Rather we have always believed that with the exception of D-notices and governmental intervention, the output is the result of the routine cultural practices of the producers, reporters and editors. Legally and conventionally such news should not happen. The real problem is how to ensure that this dominant view does not continually predominate and skew the coverage.

Annan has some useful suggestions on the strengthening of external control via a Broadcasting Complaints Commission, which would be an independent quasi-judicial body covering all cases of alleged misrepresentation or unfair treatment. This should be demanded and insisted upon by trade unionists, as should the right to monitor and analyse the output be demanded by social scientists. The public should have more control over broadcasting, with a semi-permanent Public Enquiry Board which holds public and regular hearings in a variety of regions. On both of these bodies trade union representatives should sit as of right. The assessment of broadcasting is too important to be left to the broadcasters.

The fourth television channel provides an excellent opportunity for alternative programming and a trade union news service but this possibility is unlikely. The likely outcomes and changes are probably going to be small. Raymond Williams, the cultural critic, has accurately described the report as a 'shade to the right of Matthew Arnold' and even the proposals as they stand are likely to be opposed by many, if not most, parliamentarians. However, now at last the trade union and labour movement has an evidential basis for the claims that the news is biased against it. That truth, although bad news, provides the necessary weaponry for the cultural struggle over broadcasting that is only just beginning to surface.

10

Strategies and Policies

GREG PHILO
Lecturer in Sociology, University of Glasgow

PETER BEHARRELL
Research Officer, University of Glasgow

JOHN HEWITT
Lecturer in Sociology, Liverpool College of Higher Education

It is clear that there is a growing belief amongst trade unionists that the media, and newspapers especially, are biased against them. In response, some unions have developed publicity departments, with the intention of countering the problem. There are two strategies employed in this area. One has been to develop and maintain public relations contacts with the media institutions to improve the unions' image and better the chances of getting its case across. A central priority of this strategy, then, is the improvement of personal communications with individual journalists and the extensive use of press releases. Such links with the media are obviously important. However, the strategy is rather one-sided in that it identifies the problem as being the lack of available detailed information, and the inadequate presentation of 'the facts of the case' by the unions themselves.

A second strategy has been to make complaints about particular instances of coverage by Press and broadcasting. This approach denotes a more aggressive attitude towards unfavourable journalism. It highlights the conflict of interests between unions and the media. This conflict has found its most coherent expression in the presentation of general complaints to government enquiries, such as the Royal Commission on the Press and the Annan Committee on the Future of

Broadcasting. In this context, two of the most challenging analyses of the problem of media bias have been the 'One Week' study by the A.C.T.T. in 1971, and the evidence presented by NALGO in 1975 to the Royal Commission on the Press. The important characteristic shared by these and other trade union submissions is their focus upon the problem of the *overall framework* within which industrial activities are reported.

In practice, most trade union public relations activities maintain an uneasy balance between the two strategies, seeking improved communications with journalists whilst at the same time complaining, often bitterly, about the coverage that they are actually receiving. However, there is little evidence to suggest that 'better communications' or closer working relationships between public relations departments and the media ever significantly change the character of trade union coverage. In fact, one survey of union press offices revealed many complaints about the manner in which official union statements were simply ignored (Glasgow Media Group, *Bad News*, Routledge and Kegan Paul, 1976). If taken up at all, it could still be complained that they tended to be rendered meaningless by isolation within a framework of reporting that is fundamentally hostile to the aims which trade unions represent in industrial society. The research analyses included in this volume clearly confirm this.

The severe limitations of seeking improved communications with the media have driven some unions towards a 'complaints strategy'. This is a more positive and realistic approach to the problem in that it holds few illusions about the nature of 'news' and journalistic practice within the media. But it is evident that the activities of many Press and publicity departments are not characterised by this potentially more sophisticated analysis – indeed, the response of some of the largest unions had been substantially to ignore the problem. There was no organised or ongoing strategy developed.

Whilst the T.U.C. and individual trade unions have formulated broad critiques of the media reportage of industrial life, these have tended to gather dust in the extensive volumes of evidence submitted to government commissions. In the day-to-day pursuit of a complaints strategy, individual trade unions have tended to complain about separate instances of distortion in individual newspapers. When for example the media engage in sustained and sensational coverage of an industrial dispute, trade unions have not confronted the media on the general way in which they present industry and its problems. They have not usually attacked the general practice of laying these problems at the door of trade unions. Rather, the public relations machine of individual trade unions is more usually mobilised to correct a few individual facts. Publicity departments will complain to the media that the strike record of a particular firm is not as bad as the Press or T.V. would have us believe, or that the workers have followed legitimate bargaining procedures, or that management in the firm have been intransigent, or that the media have concentrated on the effects of the dispute rather than the unionists' reasons for engaging in industrial action and so on. In doing this, the ability of the media institutions to set the agenda across whole areas of coverage and to provide the *framework* of reporting, remains unchallenged.

In practice, then, the 'complaints strategy' tends to share the problems of the 'improved communications' strategy in that whilst trade union public relations departments are aware of an *overall pattern of distortion* they have actually reacted to the media institutions, in many instances, in terms of *individual pieces of misrepresentation*.

Our own research, however, suggests that if we are to think of distortion in the media, it is not in terms of this or that individual piece of misrepresentation. Rather, the process of news production involves the systematic organisation of information around narrow and particular ways of understanding the social and industrial world. The working and social relationships of the wider society are referred to implicitly and explicitly in giving the 'news'. A knowledge of these is assumed by news journalists and is used by them to give order to news production. The information which is given thus at all times involves implicit explanations about what is happening and why. Thus, in our case study of Leyland news coverage (see Chapter 1) we found that the problems of an industry were explained as problems with the workforce. This is in part a question of some explanations being highlighted in the

coverage relative to others. More importantly, some explanations have a special significance because they are
presented in such a way that they form 'complete' explanations from within a particular view of the social world.
With this control over how the world is explained, evaluation
is implicit and there is, in fact, no need to state explicitly that
in a specific dispute the unions involved are 'wrong'. The
practical question is, how might trade unionists who object to
this situation challenge this power to define what the social
world is and when it is working 'normally'?

Our own work has provided some evidence and pointed to
the necessity of research in the area. In our view there are a
number of functions which this might serve. The first and
most concrete is to continue the work of monitoring the output
of the Press and television on a full-time basis. The importance of this is that any complaints or criticisms that individual unions or other organisations might want to make
over coverage that they have received must be based on scientific evidence and assessment. The techniques to produce this
are at present in existence but are not readily available outside
academic institutions. In truth, they are not very readily
available inside academia, since the priorities and organisation of academic funding are rarely towards anything that
might radically change or criticise the external world. It is not
at all certain that our own study, one of the few studies which
has been carried out to date, will be repeated or developed
significantly in the future. In short, if trade unions or others
wish to monitor the output of the media, then they are well advised to take a hand in financing and organising it for
themselves.

Some proposals for this are already being put forward by individual trade unions. NALGO, for example, has recently
recommended to the T.U.C. the setting up of a permanent
monitoring/research unit. In their policy document on this,
they list a number of purposes that such a unit might serve.

There seems little doubt that the establishment of a
monitoring/research unit for use by *trade unions* would be a
useful, and long overdue, development in that:

(a) A precise record of what was said and how it was presented would be available.

(b) Complaints could be based on the record.

(c) Analysis of the scrupulousness with which balance was kept could be made.

(d) Analysis of the processes through which trade union *reality* becomes trade union *news* could be made.

Such a unit would have both monitoring and research aims. The recording and storing of trade union news would be useful for all trade unions who could use the information for complaints, redress, or their own analysis.

The material would also provide an invaluable source of raw data for research purposes. Studies of process, the dynamics of news production, distortion, etc., would enrich an under-studied field and would be an invaluable asset to trade unions in their attempts to gain a wider and truer hearing for their views and policies.

To be of most use, such a unit would need to serve all trade unions and, because of the expense involved, should be set up by the TUC as a service to all affiliated unions.

Scope and details

1. A monitoring/research unit should concentrate on the national news bulletins on both radio and television.
2. Current affairs output could be sampled as and when it deals with trade union news. Also, regional output could be sampled periodically.
3. For main news output, the methods could include: keeping a note of who appears (formally or informally), alone or with others, who has statements attributed to them without appearing etc. For regional sampling, the unit might be asked by a trade union to be in the area for specific events (e.g. when there is a dispute). This latter activity would be important since much public sympathy is won or lost by local transmissions.

In addition the NALGO proposal is accompanied by a detailed cost breakdown for manning and hardware. It is certainly the most serious practical attempt so far to come to terms with the size and scope of the media institutions, and what would be required from trade unions if they were to attempt to influence media output on the basis of a scientific assessment of its content.

A second important function of such a monitoring and research unit might be the education and training of union personnel who deal with the media, such as national officials and publicity officers at district and local levels. There is much that could be done to organise more effective publicity and to exercise more control over the image that is projected of union affairs. A detailed knowledge of how the media work, what they are likely to take up as 'stories' from press releases, as well as how they interview etc., are all invaluable in this area. For example, it should be clear from all that has been said in this volume that it is not enough for trade unionists merely to state their case clearly and concisely. It is critically important in interviews, press statements and in all contacts with the media to actively attack the framework into which information about trade unions is typically fitted. In other words, if the media ask, 'Why are there so many senseless strikes?', then it is not enough to answer, 'But there aren't many' or even 'Well there has been a big drop in strikes this year'. For the very nature of the question has established that the source of the problem is to be seen in the activity of trade unionists. It is thus the question itself and the assumptions that it contains that must be attacked. These assumptions must be challenged with an alternative viewpoint, backed by critical information, which asserts the validity of a different way of understanding the social world and what is possible and desirable within it.

Such developments might be more useful if they were accompanied by attempts to work with sympathetic journalists in the media, for as it is frequently noted, people who work in the Press and television are often themselves trade unionists. Still, the possibilities in this area should not be exaggerated since there is clearly some level of control over what journalists are expected or allowed to write, as Andrew Goodman indicated (in Chapter 6 above). Stereotypical presentations and distortion are unlikely to change simply by asking people nicely.

Finally there is one other crucial dimension to research and education in this area, which emerged from the work which we undertook in trade union schools and education programmes. In the initial stages, the status of our contribution was to illustrate the process of stereotyping and distortion of trade union affairs in the media. This was intended simply as a practical guide to people who were involved in union publicity. However, as this work progressed, an important educational function for a much wider trade union audience developed. For it became apparent that the process of showing how a description of the industrial world is 'constructed', is actually to open up new ways of discussing trade union life and industrial affairs. It was frequently pointed out to us by union officers that many of their own members tended to uncritically accept the most distorted media accounts of trade union activity. Thus to show how such explanations are limited and factually incorrect is at the same time to open up the possibility of new kinds of understanding and other explanations of what is happening – for example, why there is an economic crisis and what its real causes are.

The importance of the Press and television need hardly be further emphasised – each night over twenty million people watch the news. It is not enough to say simply that they can 'make up their own minds', if we know that the information which is given is artificially limited and that it is organised and presented to involve implicit evaluations. The information which would be required for a different point of view may simply not be there. The problems which this raises for efficient trade union activity are enormous. One example which emerged from our work with NALGO was of the difficulties of organising a campaign against cuts in welfare and public expenditure if a large section of the population already believed that the crisis was caused by trade unions, strikes and 'excessive' wage claims.

A research and educational strategy which might combat this situation would, in our view, have to be formulated both locally and nationally. Locally at branch level, education programmes might be developed, linked to the work of a research and monitoring centre. The use of videotape and 'canned' educational programmes makes access to this kind of material relatively easy at a grass-roots level. In addition, a monitoring unit financed by the trade unions would further inform national policy on the mass media, its operation and its very existence might cause a serious re-thinking of the attitudes which underlie contemporary media accounts.

Appendix 1: T.U.C. Policy Proposals on the Media

The ability to regularly convey news and views on a mass scale carries with it great power to shape and direct public opinions. That much will scarcely be disputed by any interested party. Therefore the media possess great powers, potentially very dangerous to the community at large, and particularly dangerous to the interests of any class, section or group who do not have effective control over any section of the media.

Our standpoint, therefore, is clear. The public are entitled to protection from abuse of this power to influence it. Those who possess these powers must be required to exercise them within the terms of an 'operator's licence'. The qualification for holding such a licence must be the acceptance and practice of clearly defined standards of responsibility and accountability.

Speech by Mostyn Evans, national organiser of T.G.W.U., given to T.U.C. Conference on Trade Unions and the Media, 17 February 1977.

The T.U.C. policy proposals are as follows:

1. A continuous check on the ownership and control of all newspapers, magazines, radio and television networks, to prevent any further concentration, to publicise all interlocking interests, and actively to promote dispersion of ownership and control.

The necessary committee would be responsible for advising government on any subsidy seen to be required to preserve a viable and free Press, and for continuously reviewing the economic situation in the industry.

2. To give large and representative groups in society, such as the trade union movement, the positive opportunity to

enter the national newspaper publishing field, through a National Press Finance Corporation. This N.P.F.C. would receive all advertising revenues, and deduct a levy before passing such revenues on to recipients. Such a system would minimise the opportunity for large advertisers to dictate editorial policy in any section of the media, and would provide the means for the N.P.F.C. to buy printing plant, which could be leased to representative interest groups with the capacity to sustain a major publishing venture. This corporation would be empowered to control the proportion of advertising to editorial material in all sections of the media.

3. To maintain a continuous monitoring of all material issued through all aspects of the media, in order to have the means to check, and verify or disprove, in a detailed fashion, any complaint of lack of balance, distortion, invasion of privacy etc.

4. A capacity to ensure the full immediate and public investigation of all such complaints, and the full, immediate action necessary to correct any misleading information or to redress any lack of balance.

5. A responsibility, exercised through a committee of employers and trade union representatives from within the industry, to pursue good industrial relations in the industry, through full recognition of trade union rights at all levels, and the active encouragement of industrial democracy in the industry.

Appendix 2: N.U.J. Code of Conduct

The National Union of Journalists' Code of Conduct provides valuable standards for Press freedom, and is backed by disciplinary powers. The Code is an implicit indictment of much that appears in the mass media.

1. A journalist has a duty to maintain the highest professional and ethical standards.

2. A journalist shall at all times defend the principle of the freedom of the Press and other media in relation to the collection of information and the expression of comment and criticism. He/she shall strive to eliminate distortion, news suppression and censorship.

3. A journalist shall strive to ensure that the information he/she disseminates is fair and accurate, avoid the expression of comment and conjecture as established fact and falsification by distortion, selection or misrepresentation.

4. A journalist shall rectify promptly any harmful inaccuracies, ensure that corrections and apologies receive due prominence and afford the right of reply to persons criticised when the issue is of sufficient importance.

5. A journalist shall obtain information, photographs and illustrations only by straightforward means. The use of other means can be justified only by over-riding considerations of public interest. The journalist is entitled to exercise a personal conscientious objection to the use of such means.

6. Subject to justification by over-riding considerations of the public interest, a journalist shall do nothing which entails the intrusion into private grief and distress.

7. A journalist shall protect confidential sources of information.

8. A journalist shall not accept bribes nor shall he/she

allow other inducements to influence the performance of his/her professional duties.

9. A journalist shall not lend himself/herself to the distortion or suppression of the truth because of advertising or other considerations.

10. A journalist shall not originate material which encourages discrimination on grounds of race, colour, creed, gender or sexual orientation.

11. A journalist shall not take private advantage of information gained in the course of his/her duties, before the information is public knowledge.

Notes on Contributors

FRANCIS BECKETT worked for the N.U.S. for four years as manager of the publicity department, Press officer and editor of *National Student* the Union's newspaper. He is an elected member of the N.U.J. Executive, and is chairman of the N.U.J.'s P.R. and Development Committee.

PETER BEHARRELL is Research Officer at the University of Glasgow, and as a member of the Glasgow Media Group is co-author of *Bad News* (Routledge and Kegan Paul, 1976) and *More Bad News* (to be published 1977).

J. BROOKE CRUTCHLEY is Senior Lecturer in Sociology at Middlesex Polytechnic.

HOWARD DAVIS is Lecturer in Sociology at the University of Kent, Canterbury. A member of the Glasgow Media Group, he is co-author of *Bad News* and *More Bad News*.

PETER GOLDING is Research Fellow at the Centre for Mass Communications Research, University of Leicester. He is the author of *The Mass Media* (Longman, 1974) and has written articles on the media and communications.

ANDREW GOODMAN joined the B.B.C. as a trainee in 1966 and worked there as a production assistant and producer until 1971. He has worked as a producer for Yorkshire T.V., as T.V. critic for *Time Out* magazine and is now a freelance producer in television and for the Australian Broadcasting Commission in radio.

TONI GRIFFITHS began work as a journalist on the *Western Mail* in Cardiff before moving to the N.U.T. as publicity assistant. Since then she has worked as Press Officer for the National Foundation for Educational Research, the National Children's Bureau and is now Press Officer at NALGO.

JOHN HEWITT is Lecturer in Sociology at Liverpool College of Higher Education. He is co-author with the other members of the Glasgow Media Group of *Bad News* and *More Bad News*.

TONY MARSHALL has worked for the last four years at the Publicity and Research Department of N.U.A.A.W., where he is deputy editor of the union's journal *Landworker*.

GRAHAM MURDOCK is Research Fellow at the Centre for Mass Communications Research, University of Leicester. He is the author of numerous articles on the political economy of the mass media and on popular culture.

GREG PHILO is Lecturer in Sociology at the University of Glasgow. With the other members of the Glasgow Media Group he is co-author of *Bad News* and *More Bad News*.

ALAN SAPPER is General Secretary of the Association of Cinematograph Television and Allied Technicians.

PAUL WALTON is Senior Lecturer in Sociology at the University of Glasgow. He is co-author (with Andrew Gamble) of *From Alienation to Surplus Value* (Sheed and Ward, 1972), *The New Criminology* (with Jock Young and Ian Taylor, Routledge and Kegan Paul, 1973), and with Andrew Gamble *Capitalism in Crisis* (Macmillan, 1976). He is co-author with the other members of the Glasgow Media Group of *Bad News* and *More Bad News*.

JOCK YOUNG is Principal Lecturer in Sociology at Middlesex Polytechnic. He is the author of *The Drugtakers* (Paladin, 1971) and co-author (with Paul Walton and Ian Taylor) of *The New Criminology*. He edited (with Stan Cohen) a reader on mass communications, *The Manufacture of News* (Constable, 1973).

Bibliography

HISTORICAL STUDIES OF PRESS AND COMMUNICATIONS

Febvre, H. and Martin, H., *The Coming of the Book* (New Left Books, 1976).

Hollis, P., *The Pauper Press* (Oxford University Press, 1970).

Thompson, E. P., *The Making of the English Working Class* (Pelican, 1968).

Webb, R. K., *The British Working Class Reader* (Allen & Unwin, 1955).

Williams, R., *The Long Revolution* (Penguin, 1965).

CONTEMPORARY STUDIES

Cohen, S., *Folk Devils and Moral Panics* (Paladin, 1973).

Cohen, S. (ed.), *Images of Deviance* (Penguin, 1971).

Cohen, S. and Young, J. (eds), *The Manufacture of News* (Constable, 1973).

Collins, R., *Television News* (British Film Institute, Television Monograph 5, London 1976).

Elliot, P., *The Making of a Television Series* (Constable, 1972).

Enzensberger, H. M., *The Consciousness Industry* (Seabury Press, New York, 1974).

Enzensberger, H. M., 'Constituents of a Theory of the Media' *New Left Review*, 64 (Nov – Dec 1970).

Glasgow University Media Group, *Bad News* (Routledge and Kegan Paul, 1976).

Glasgow University Media Group, *More Bad News* (Routledge and Kegan Paul, 1977).

Hall, S., 'A World at One with Itself' and 'The Determination of News Photographs' in Cohen and Young (eds) *The Manufacture of News*, op. cit.

Halloran, J., Elliot, P. and Murdock, G., *Demonstrations and Communications: A Case Study* (Penguin, 1970).

Husband, C., *White Media, Black Britain* (Arrow, 1976).

McCann, E., 'The British Press and Northern Ireland' in Cohen and Young (eds) *The Manufacture of News*, op. cit.

Miliband, R., *The State in Capitalist Society* (Basic Books, New York, 1969).

Morley, D., 'Industrial Conflict and The Mass Media', *Sociological Review*, vol. 24, no. 2 (May 1976).

Murdock, G., 'Mass Communications and the Construction of Meaning' in Armistead N. *Reconstructing Social Psychology* (Penguin, 1974).

Murdock, G. and Golding, P., 'Capitalism, Communications and Class Relations' in Curran, J. *et al.* (eds) *Mass Communications and Society* (Edward Arnold, London, 1977).

Murdock, G. and Golding, P., 'The Political Economy of the Mass Media' in Miliband and Saville (eds) *Socialist Register* (Merlin Press, 1973).

Pateman, T., *Language, Truth and Politics* (Published by Jean Stroud and T. Pateman, 1975).

Pateman, T., *Television and the February 1974 General Election* (British Film Institute Television Monograph 3, London, 1974).

Robinson, T., *National Newspapers: the End or a New Beginning?* (Workers' Educational Association Background Notes no. S.S.26, 1976).